studysync®

Reading & Writing Companion

Highs and Lows

What do we learn from love and loss?

studysync.com

Send all inquiries to:
BookheadEd Learning, LLC
610 Daniel Young Drive
Sonoma, CA 95476

ISBN 978-1-94-469580-4

4 5 6 7 8 9 LMN 24 23 22 21 20

B

Student Guide

Getting Started

Welcome to the StudySync Reading & Writing Companion! In this book, you will find a collection of readings based on the theme of the unit you are studying. As you work through the readings, you will be asked to answer questions and perform a variety of tasks designed to help you closely analyze and understand each text selection. Read on for an explanation of each

Close Reading and Writing Routine

In each unit, you will read texts that share a common theme, despite their different genres, time periods, and authors. Each reading encourages a closer look through questions and a short writing assignment.

Rikki-Tikki-Tavi
FICTION
Rudyard Kipling
1894

1 Introduction

studysync●

"**R**ikki-Tikki-Tavi" is one of the most famous tales from *The Jungle Book*, a collection of short stories published in 1894 by English author Rudyard Kipling (1865–1936). The stories in *The Jungle Book* feature animal characters with anthropomorphic traits and are intended to be read as fables, each illustrating a moral lesson. In this story, Rikki-tikki-tavi is a courageous young mongoose adopted as a pet by a British family living in 19th-century colonial India.

Rikki-Tikki-Tavi

"Rikki-tikki held on with his eyes shut, for now he was quite sure he was dead."

This is the story of the great war that Rikki-tikki-tavi fought single-handed, through the bath-rooms of the big bungalow in Segowlee cantonment. Darzee, the Tailorbird, helped him, and Chuchundra, the musk-rat, who never comes out into the middle of the floor, but always creeps round by the wall, gave him advice, but Rikki-tikki did the real fighting.

He was a mongoose, rather like a little cat in his fur and his tail, but quite like a weasel in his head and his habits. His eyes and the end of his restless nose were pink. He could scratch himself anywhere he pleased with any leg, front or back, that he chose to use. He could fluff up his tail till it looked like a bottle brush, and his war cry as he scuttled through the long grass was: "Rikk-tikk-tikki-tikki-tchk!"

One day, a high summer flood washed him out of the burrow where he lived with his father and mother, and carried him, kicking and clucking, down a roadside ditch. He found a little wisp of grass floating there, and clung to it till he lost his senses. When he revived, he was lying in the hot sun on the middle of a garden path, very draggled indeed, and a small boy was saying, "Here's a dead mongoose. Let's have a funeral."

"No," said his mother, "let's take him in and dry him. Perhaps he isn't really dead."

They took him into the house, and a big man picked him up between his finger and thumb and said he was not dead but half choked. So they wrapped him in cotton wool, and warmed him over a little fire, and he opened his eyes and sneezed.

"Now," said the big man (he was an Englishman who had just moved into the bungalow), "don't frighten him, and we'll see what he'll do."

 Skill
Textual Evidence

It says that he fluffs up his tail and he has a war cry. I know that a war cry is used in battle to rally the troops. This must mean that Rikki-tikki is brave and powerful, like a soldier.

 Skill
Text-Dependent Responses

After finding Rikki-tikki, the English family brought him into their home and took care of him.

1 Introduction

An Introduction to each text provides historical context for your reading as well as information about the author. You will also learn about the genre of the text and the year in which it was written.

2 Notes

Many times, while working through the activities after each text, you will be asked to **annotate** or **make annotations** about what you are reading. This means that you should highlight or underline words in the text and use the "Notes" column to make comments or jot down any questions you have. You may also want to note any unfamiliar vocabulary words here.

You will also see sample student annotations to go along with the Skill lesson for that text.

Reading & Writing Companion

③ First Read

During your first reading of each selection, you should just try to get a general idea of the content and message of the reading. Don't worry if there are parts you don't understand or words that are unfamiliar to you. You'll have an opportunity later to dive deeper into the text.

④ Think Questions

These questions will ask you to start thinking critically about the text, asking specific questions about its purpose, and making connections to your prior knowledge and reading experiences. To answer these questions, you should go back to the text and draw upon specific evidence to support your responses. You will also begin to explore some of the more challenging vocabulary words in the selection.

⑤ Skills

Each Skill includes two parts: Checklist and Your Turn. In the Checklist, you will learn the process for analyzing the text. The model student annotations in the text provide examples of how you might make your own notes following the instructions in the Checklist. In the Your Turn, you will use those same instructions to practice the skill.

---

③ RIKKI-TIKKI-TAVI First Read
studysync

Read "Rikki-Tikki-Tavi." After you read, complete the Think Questions below.

④ ☁ THINK QUESTIONS

1. How did Rikki-tikki come to live with the English family? Cite specific evidence from the text to support your answer.

2. What do the descriptions of Nag and the dialogue in paragraphs 23–24 suggest about Nag's character? Cite specific evidence from the text to support your answer.

3. Describe in two to three sentences how Rikki-tikki saves the family from snakes.

4. Find the word **cultivated** in paragraph 18 of "Rikki-Tikki-Tavi." Use context clues in the surrounding sentences, as well as the sentence in which the word appears, to determine the word's meaning. Write your definition here and identify clues that helped you figure out the word's meaning.

5. Use context clues to determine the meaning of **sensible** as it is used in paragraph 79 of "Rikki-Tikki-Tavi." Write your definition of *sensible* here and identify clues that helped you figure out the meaning. Then check the meaning in the dictionary.

---

⑤ CHARACTER — Skill: Character

Use the Checklist to analyze Character in "Rikki-Tikki-Tavi." Refer to the sample student annotations about Character in the text.

••• CHECKLIST FOR CHARACTER

In order to determine how particular elements of a story or drama interact, note the following:

✓ the characters in the story, including the protagonist and antagonist
✓ the settings and how they shape the characters or plot
✓ plot events and how they affect the characters
✓ key events or series of episodes in the plot, especially events that cause characters to react, respond, or change in some way
✓ characters' responses as the plot reaches a climax and moves toward a resolution of the problem facing the protagonist
✓ the resolution of the conflict in the plot and the ways that affects each character

To analyze how particular elements of a story or drama interact, consider the following questions:

✓ How do the characters' responses change or develop from the beginning to the end of the story?
✓ How does the setting shape the characters and plot in the story?
✓ How do the events in the plot affect the characters? How do they develop as a result of the conflict, climax, and resolution?
✓ Do the characters' problems reach a resolution? How?

⟳ YOUR TURN

1. How does the mother's love for her son affect her actions in paragraph 37?

   ○ A. It prompts her to keep her son away from Rikki-tikki.
   ○ B. It causes a disagreement between her and her husband.
   ○ C. It makes her show affection towards Rikki-tikki.
   ○ D. It makes Rikki-tikki feel nervous staying with the family.

2. What does the dialogue in paragraph 40 suggest about Chuchundra?

   ○ A. He is afraid.
   ○ B. He is easily fooled.
   ○ C. He is optimistic.
   ○ D. He loves Rikki-tikki.

3. Which paragraph shows that Teddy looks to Rikki-tikki for protection?

   ○ A. 37
   ○ B. 38
   ○ C. 39
   ○ D. 40

Close Read

RIKKI-TIKKI-TAVI
studysync●

Close Read

⑥

Reread "Rikki-Tikki-Tavi." As you reread, complete the Skills Focus questions below. Then use your answers and annotations from the questions to help you complete the Write activity.

◎ SKILLS FOCUS

1. Identify details that reveal Nag's character when he is first introduced in the story. Explain what inferences you can make about Nag and what makes him a threat.

2. Identify details that reveal Rikki-tikki's character traits as a fighter. Explain how those character traits help Rikki-tikki defeat the snakes.

3. Find examples of Nag and Nagaina's actions and dialogue. How do their words and behaviors create conflict in the plot?

4. Identify details that help you compare and contrast Rikki-tikki and Darzee. Explain what you can infer about Rikki-tikki and Darzee from these details.

5. Analyze details that show how Rikki-tikki beats the snakes. Explain Rikki-tikki's approach to conflict.

✎ WRITE

⑦

LITERARY ANALYSIS: In this classic story of good vs. evil, Nag and Nagaina are portrayed as the villains. Consider the role and behaviors of the typical villain. Then think about Nag and Nagaina's behaviors, including how they impact the plot and interact with other characters. Do you think that Nag and Nagaina are truly evil, or have they been unfairly cast as villains? Choose a side, and write a brief response explaining your position and analysis. Use several pieces of textual evidence to support your points.

Reading & Writing Companion 21

Ready for Marcos
FICTION

Introduction

Twelve-year-old Monica Alvarez has a happy life. She is a star on the track team and has many good friends. But everything changes when her parents bring Marcos, her new baby brother, home from the hospital. Her parents want her to have more responsibilities. Monica wonders what it will mean to be a big sister. Is she ready? Is she willing?

■ VOCABULARY

vivacious
energetic and happy; lively

justify
to support with good reasons

covertly
done in secret

subtle
barely noticeable

---

⑥

Close Read & Skills Focus

After you have completed the First Read, you will be asked to go back and read the text more closely and critically. Before you begin your Close Read, you should read through the Skills Focus to get an idea of the concepts you will want to focus on during your second reading. You should work through the Skills Focus by making annotations, highlighting important concepts, and writing notes or questions in the "Notes" column. Depending on instructions from your teacher, you may need to respond online or use a separate piece of paper to start expanding on your thoughts and ideas.

⑦

Write

Your study of each selection will end with a writing assignment. For this assignment, you should use your notes, annotations, personal ideas, and answers to both the Think and Skills Focus questions. Be sure to read the prompt carefully and address each part of it in your writing.

⑧

English Language Learner

The English Language Learner texts focus on improving language proficiency. You will practice learning strategies and skills in individual and group activities to become better readers, writers, and speakers.

Extended Writing Project and Grammar

This is your opportunity to use genre characteristics and craft to compose meaningful, longer written works exploring the theme of each unit. You will draw information from your readings, research, and own life experiences to complete the assignment.

1 Writing Project

After you have read all of the unit text selections, you will move on to a writing project. Each project will guide you through the process of writing your essay. Student models will provide guidance and help you organize your thoughts. One unit ends with an **Extended Oral Project,** which will give you an opportunity to develop your oral language and communication skills.

2 Writing Process Steps

There are four steps in the writing process: Plan, Draft, Revise, and Edit and Publish. During each step, you will form and shape your writing project, and each lesson's peer review will give you the chance to receive feedback from your peers and teacher.

3 Writing Skills

Each Skill lesson focuses on a specific strategy or technique that you will use during your writing project. Each lesson presents a process for applying the skill to your own work and gives you the opportunity to practice it to improve your writing.

1 Extended Writing Project and Grammar

Extended Writing Project and Grammar

2 Narrative Writing Process: Plan

| PLAN | DRAFT | REVISE | EDIT AND PUBLISH |

Extended Writing Project and Grammar

3 Skill: Organizing Narrative Writing

••• CHECKLIST FOR ORGANIZING NARRATIVE WRITING

As you consider how to organize your narrative, use the following questions as a guide:

- Who is the narrator and who are the characters in the story?
- From what point of view will the story be told?
- Where will the story take place?
- What conflict or problem will the characters have to resolve?
- Does my plot flow logically and naturally from one event to the next?

Highs and Lows

What do we learn from love and loss?

Genre Focus: POETRY

Texts

 Paired Readings

Extended Writing Project and Grammar

What do we learn from love and loss?

CHARLES DICKENS

Novelist, journalist, and critic Charles Dickens (1812–1870) was born in Portsmouth, England. At the age of twelve, his father was sent to debtors' prison, and Dickens left school to work ten-hour days in a factory. These experiences informed his later work, including *Oliver Twist, A Christmas Carol, David Copperfield,* and *Great Expectations.* In total, he wrote fifteen novels, five novellas, hundreds of short stories, and he edited a journal published weekly for twenty years.

ALBERT MARRIN

Albert Marrin (b. 1936) is a graduate of City College of New York and Yeshiva University, where he is a professor of history. His career as an author began while teaching in the East Bronx when he used "storytime" to engage students and tell tales like "Custer's Last Stand." His first book, *War and the Christian Conscience: From Augustine to Martin Luther King, Jr.,* was written for an adult audience, but, missing "storytime," he went on to write three dozen young adult books, beginning in 1982 with his first, *Overlord: D-Day* and the *Invasion of Europe.*

ALFRED NOYES

Alfred Noyes (1880–1958) was born in Wolverhampton, England, and attended Exeter College, Oxford, but did not finish his degree; he missed his finals in 1903 to meet with a publisher for his first volume of poetry, *The Loom of Years,* which received favorable reviews from W. B. Yeats. Over the next five years, he published five books of poetry, as well as two of his most famous poems, "The Highwayman" and "Drake." He went on to write novels as well as literary criticism, a trilogy of poems called *The Torch-Bearers,* and to teach at Princeton University.

EDGAR ALLAN POE

Edgar Allan Poe (1809–1849) was born in Boston, Massachusetts. He was orphaned after his mother Elizabeth died, and he was taken in by John and Frances Allan of Richmond, Virginia. Poe went on to attend the University of Virginia, but left after a year because of problems coming up with his tuition. He then enlisted in the army and attended West Point until he intentionally got himself court-martialed, at which point he focused on writing. At thirty-five, he broke through when his poem "The Raven" was published to instant success. He died five years later in Baltimore.

SUSAN POWER

A member of the Standing Rock Tribe of the Dakotas, Susan Power (b. 1961) was born in Chicago, Illinois. She received degrees from Harvard/Radcliffe University and Harvard Law School. She decided to end her law career and become a writer after having a vision while recovering from an appendectomy. She saw a Dakota Sioux woman standing in her hospital room, who would go on to be a main character in her first novel, *The Grass Dancer,* which won the PEN/Hemingway Award for a First Novel in 1995.

TERESA PALOMO ACOSTA

Born in McGregor, Texas, Teresa Palomo Acosta (b. 1949) is a poet, historian, author, and activist, whose work sheds light on the underrepresented narratives and histories of Mexican American communities in Texas. Both of Acosta's parents were descendants of Mexican migrant workers who settled in Central Texas in the 1930s, and much of her work draws inspiration from this heritage. With Ruthe Winegarten, she co-authored *Las Tejanas: 300 Years of History* about the often-overlooked contributions of Mexican American women to Texas history. Acosta has lived and worked in Austin, Texas, since the late 1970s.

EDWARD BLOOR

Edward Bloor (b. 1950), author of *Tangerine*, was born in Trenton, New Jersey. Bloor worked as high school English teacher before becoming an editor for a major publishing house. During his time there, he wrote several books. On his transition from editor to writer, Bloor said, "My teaching job led to a job in educational publishing, where I was actually required to sit and read young adult novels all day long. So I decided to try it myself." He lives in Winter Garden, Florida.

MARCELA FUENTES

Marcela Fuentes grew up in South Texas, graduated from the University of Texas at Austin, and attended the Iowa Writers' Workshop. She's been published in the *Indiana Review, Bodega Magazine, Blackbird, Stoneslide Corrective, Juked*, and *Vestal Review*. She currently teaches at Texas A&M University as an assistant professor of creative writing and Latinx literature.

ARACELIS GIRMAY

Aracelis Girmay (b. 1977) was born and raised in Orange County, California, attended Connecticut College, and earned her MFA from New York University. She is the author of *Teeth and Kingdom Animalia,* in addition to a collage-based book, *changing, changing*. Girmay's work covers the territory between memory and loss, and what it means to be a citizen in the 21st century. Her poem "Noche de Lluvia, San Salvador" was featured as part of the New York City subway's Poetry in Motion program. She teaches at Hampshire College and Drew University in New Jersey.

WING TEK LUM

Wing Tek Lum (b. 1946) was born in Honolulu, Hawaii. At Brown University, he studied engineering and became an editor of the school's literary journal. He helped organize against the Vietnam War, and was arrested at the Pentagon for protesting. From there, he went to Union Theological Seminary, graduated with a Master of Divinity, and eventually became a social worker. He is the author of two books of poetry, *Expounding the Doubtful Points* and *The Nanjing Massacre: Poems*. He lives in Hawaii.

ALEX SHULTZ

Alex Shultz has written for *Grantland, SLAM, Los Angeles Magazine*, and the *Los Angeles Times*. Raised in Plano, Texas, Shultz studied print and digital journalism at the University of Southern California, where he began writing at the *Daily Trojan* before becoming a sports editor. He lives in Brooklyn, New York, and works as a freelance journalist.

Annabel Lee

POETRY
Edgar Allan Poe
1849

Introduction

Edgar Allan Poe's (1809–1849) last complete poem, "Annabel Lee," follows a familiar Poe storyline—the death of a beautiful woman. Poe lost many women close to him over the course of his life, and there has been much speculation and debate about who served as the inspiration for the heroine of this poem. Most people believe that Poe wrote the poem about his late wife, Virginia Clemm, who

". . . we loved with a love that was more than love— I and my Annabel Lee—"

1   It was many and many a year ago,
2   In a kingdom by the sea,
3   That a maiden there lived whom you may know
4   By the name of Annabel Lee;
5   And this maiden she lived with no other thought
6   Than to love and be loved by me.

7   *I* was a child and *she* was a child,
8   In this kingdom by the sea,
9   But we loved with a love that was more than love—
10   I and my Annabel Lee—
11 With a love that the wingèd **seraphs** of Heaven
12   **Coveted** her and me.

13 And this was the reason that, long ago,
14   In this kingdom by the sea,
15 A wind blew out of a cloud, chilling
16   My beautiful Annabel Lee;
17 So that her highborn[1] **kinsmen** came
18   And bore her away from me,
19 To shut her up in a **sepulchre**
20   In this kingdom by the sea.

21 The angels, not half so happy in Heaven,
22   Went envying[2] her and me—
23   Yes!—that was the reason (as all men know,
24   In this kingdom by the sea)
25 That the wind came out of the cloud by night,
26   Chilling and killing my Annabel Lee.

---

1. **highborn** referring to someone of noble birth, such as a lord, a lady, or a knight
2. **envying** feeling jealous of something

Virginia Clemm Poe, Edgar Allan Poe's wife, died at the age of 23. Her death is believed to have affected and inspired Poe's writing, including the poem "Annabel Lee."

 NOTES

 Skill: Media

The video begins with a song that is spooky and romantic. The first few lines sound mostly romantic. The sad and spooky parts come later. The music helps me understand right away that this is a sad love poem.

 Skill: Figurative Language

The narrator mentions the seraphs in Heaven. This is a reference to the Bible, where seraphs are a type of angel. This makes it sound like their love is the most powerful and sacred thing because it makes even angels jealous.

Skill:
Poetic Elements
and Structure

In the fourth stanza I
see a pattern created
by mixing short and
long lines. Only the
shorter lines rhyme.
The meter is uneven
and makes me feel like
I'm swaying. This part
makes me feel uneasy
and sad, as if it can't
keep going. It fits in
with the tragedy of
Annabel's death.

27 But our love it was stronger by far than the love
28   Of those who were older than we—
29   Of many far wiser than we—
30 And neither the angels in Heaven above
31   Nor the demons down under the sea
32 Can ever **dissever** my soul from the soul
33   Of the beautiful Annabel Lee;

34 For the moon never beams, without bringing me dreams
35   Of the beautiful Annabel Lee;
36 And the stars never rise, but I feel the bright eyes
37   Of the beautiful Annabel Lee;
38 And so, all the night-tide[3], I lie down by the side
39   Of my darling—my darling—my life and my bride,
40   In her sepulchre there by the sea—
41   In her tomb by the sounding sea.

---

3. **night-tide** an old-fashioned or literary way of saying "nighttime"

  Reading & Writing
Companion

First Read

Read "Annabel Lee." After you read, complete the Think Questions below.

 THINK QUESTIONS

1. What is the relationship between the speaker of the poem and Annabel Lee? Cite textual evidence from the poem to support your answer.

2. What happens to Annabel Lee? Cite textual evidence from the poem to support your answer.

3. Write two to three sentences describing how the speaker is affected by his relationship with Annabel Lee. Cite evidence from the text to support your answer.

4. Find the word **coveted** in line 12 of "Annabel Lee." Use context clues in the surrounding lines, as well as the line in which the word appears, to determine the word's meaning. Write your definition here and identify clues that helped you figure out the meaning.

5. Use context clues to determine the meaning of **dissever** as it is used in line 32 of "Annabel Lee." Write your definition here and identify clues that helped you figure out the meaning. Then check the meaning in a dictionary.

Reading & Writing Companion

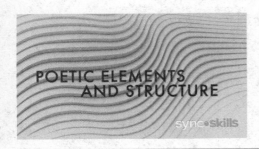

Skill:
Poetic Elements and Structure

Use the Checklist to analyze Poetic Elements and Structure in "Annabel Lee." Refer to the sample student annotations about Poetic Elements and Structure in the text.

••• CHECKLIST FOR POETIC ELEMENTS AND STRUCTURE

In order to identify sound elements chosen by the poet, note the following:

✓ the rhyme, rhythm, and meter, if present

✓ lines and stanzas in the poem that suggest its meaning

✓ other sound elements, such as:

- alliteration: the repetition of initial consonant sounds, as with the *s* sound in "Cindy sweeps the sand"

- consonance: the repetition of consonant sounds in the middle and ends of words, as with the *t* sound in "little bats in the attic"

- assonance: the repetition of vowel sounds in words, as with the long *e* sound in "dreams of bees and sheep"

✓ lines or whole stanzas can be arranged to have a specific effect on the reader

To analyze the impact of rhymes and other repetitions of sounds on a specific verse or stanza of a poem, consider the following questions:

✓ What sound elements are present in specific stanzas of the poem?

✓ What is the effect of different sound elements on the stanza or verse?

✓ How do the sound elements emphasize important ideas or the poem's meaning?

Skill:
Poetic Elements and Structure

Reread lines 34–41 of "Annabel Lee." Then, using the Checklist on the previous page, answer the multiple-choice questions below.

🔁 YOUR TURN

1. What is unusual about the rhymes in lines 34, 36, and 38?

   ○ A. Each line has a word within it that rhymes with its last word.

   ○ B. The lines rhyme with one another.

   ○ C. The rhyming words in these lines all have different vowel sounds.

   ○ D. The rhyming words all end with the sound of the letter *s*.

2. What is the impact of the rhyme scheme in lines 34, 36, and 38 on the stanza?

   ○ A. The rhyme scheme creates a dreamy and light feeling.

   ○ B. The rhyme scheme creates a harsh and angry feeling.

   ○ C. The rhyme scheme has no effect at all.

   ○ D. The rhyme scheme creates an uneasy feeling.

Skill:
Figurative Language

Use the Checklist to analyze Figurative Language in "Annabel Lee." Refer to the sample student annotations about Figurative Language in the text.

••• CHECKLIST FOR FIGURATIVE LANGUAGE

To identify figures of speech and figurative language in a text, note the following:

- ✓ words that mean one thing literally and suggest something else

- ✓ similes, such as "strong as an ox" or metaphors, such as "her eyes were stars"

- ✓ personification, such as "the daisies danced in the wind"

- ✓ allusions, or indirect references, to people, texts, events, or ideas, such as

  - biblical allusions, such as describing a beautiful place as "The Garden of Eden"
  - mythological allusions, such as describing a strong character as "Herculean"
  - literary allusions, such as calling someone who likes romance "a real Romeo"

In order to interpret the meaning of a figure of speech in context, ask the following questions:

- ✓ Does any of the descriptive language in the text compare two seemingly unlike things?

- ✓ Do any descriptions include "like" or "as," indicating a simile?

- ✓ Is there a direct comparison that suggests a metaphor?

- ✓ Is a human quality used to describe an animal, object, force of nature, or idea?

- ✓ What literary, biblical, or mythological allusions do you recognize?

- ✓ How does this figure of speech change your understanding of the thing or person being described?

To analyze the impact of figurative language on a text's meaning, use these questions as a guide:

- ✓ Where does figurative language appear in the text? What does it mean?

- ✓ Why does the author use figurative language rather than literal language?

Skill:
Figurative Language

Reread lines 27–33 of "Annabel Lee." Then, using the Checklist on the previous page, answer the multiple-choice questions below.

⟳ YOUR TURN

1. What is the biblical allusion in this stanza?

   ○ A. our love was stronger by far
   ○ B. Of those who were older than we / Of many far wiser
   ○ C. neither the angels in Heaven above / Nor the demons down under the sea
   ○ D. dissever my soul from the soul / Of the beautiful Annabel Lee

2. What is the effect of the allusion in this stanza?

   ○ A. It suggests that death is confusing and upsetting because both good and evil biblical creatures are against Annabel Lee and the speaker in the poem.
   ○ B. It supports the central idea that the forces of good will always support true love because the angels helped Annabel Lee and the narrator in the poem.
   ○ C. It builds a suspenseful tone by implying a fight between good and evil.
   ○ D. It makes the sound of the poem mirror the dying heartbeat of Annabel Lee.

Please note that excerpts and passages in the StudySync® library and this workbook are intended as touchstones to generate interest in an author's work. The excerpts and passages do not substitute for the reading of entire texts, and StudySync® strongly recommends that students seek out and purchase the whole literary or informational work in order to experience it as the author intended. Links to online resellers are available in our digital library. In addition, complete works may be ordered through an authorized reseller by filling out and returning to StudySync® the order form enclosed in this workbook.

Reading & Writing Companion

7

Skill:
Media

Use the Checklist to analyze Media in "Annabel Lee." Refer to the sample student annotations about Media in the text.

••• CHECKLIST FOR MEDIA

In order to determine how to compare and contrast a written story, drama, or poem to its audio, filmed, staged, or multimedia version, do the following:

✓ choose a story that has been presented in multiple forms of media, such as a written story and a film adaptation

✓ note techniques that are unique to each medium—print, audio, and video:

- sound
- music
- tone and style
- word choice
- structure

✓ examine how these techniques may have an effect on the story and its ideas, as well as the reader's, listener's, or viewer's understanding of the work as a whole

✓ examine similarities and differences between the written story and its audio or video versions

To compare and contrast a written story, drama, or poem to its audio, filmed, staged, or multimedia version, analyzing the effects of techniques unique to each medium, consider the following questions:

✓ How do different types of media treat story elements?

✓ What techniques are unique to each medium—print, audio, and video?

✓ How does the medium—for example, a film's use of music, sound, and camera angles—affect a person's understanding of the work as a whole?

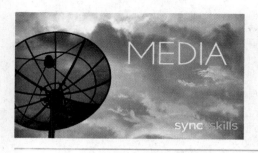

Skill:
Media

Reread lines 17–26 of "Annabel Lee" and then view this same scene in the video. Then, using the Checklist on the previous page, answer the multiple-choice questions below.

⟳ YOUR TURN

1. This question has two parts. First, answer Part A. Then, answer Part B.

   Part A: What sound element helps support the tone of the poem?

   ○ A. The sound effects of birds
   ○ B. The music gets louder.
   ○ C. The gate clangs on the sepulchre.
   ○ D. The music turns happy.

   Part B: What effect does the sound element in Part A have on the poem?

   ○ A. It helps build tension.
   ○ B. It makes it easier to picture what is happening.
   ○ C. It helps make the poem feel romantic.
   ○ D. It helps me understand what happened to Annabel Lee.

Please note that excerpts and passages in the StudySync® library and this workbook are intended as touchstones to generate interest in an author's work. The excerpts and passages do not substitute for the reading of entire texts, and StudySync® strongly recommends that students seek out and purchase the whole literary or informational work in order to experience it as the author intended. Links to online resellers are available in our digital library. In addition, complete works may be ordered through an authorized reseller by filling out and returning to StudySync® the order form enclosed in this workbook.

Reading & Writing
Companion

9

Close Read

Reread "Annabel Lee." As you reread, complete the Skills Focus questions below. Then use your answers and annotations from the questions to help you complete the Write activity.

◎ SKILLS FOCUS

1. Identify details that show how the speaker feels about Annabel Lee before and after her death.

2. Identify the rhyme and rhythm in the fifth stanza of the poem. Explain how these poetic elements emphasize the speaker's feelings.

3. The speaker makes several biblical allusions to both angels and demons. What might this suggest about the speaker's feelings or the meaning of the poem?

4. How did the multimedia version use sound elements to emphasize the speaker's feelings or meaning of the poem? Identify and explain one or two examples.

5. Reread the last stanza. Identify details that show how the speaker feels now that his deepest relationship has been lost.

✏ WRITE

LITERARY ANALYSIS: How did Poe use rhyme, rhythm, and allusions to help the reader understand how the speaker feels about Annabel Lee? How did the multimedia version use sound to emphasize these same feelings? Write a short response to this question. Remember to use specific examples from the poem and the multimedia version to support your response.

My Mother Pieced Quilts

POETRY
Teresa Palomo Acosta
1976

Introduction

Teresa Palomo Acosta (b. 1949) is a Tejana author, activist, and historian born in McGregor, Texas. The daughter of working-class parents who came to Texas during the Great Depression, Acosta spent much of her youth in and around cotton fields, listening to her family's stories and watching the women sew. In her poem "My Mother Pieced Quilts," Acosta describes in verse how her mother would stitch various pieces of fabric into beautiful quilts, each one summoning its

"oh mother you plunged me sobbing and laughing into our past"

1 they were just meant as covers
2 in winters
3 as weapons
4 against pounding january winds

5 but it was just that every morning I awoke to these
6 october **ripened** canvases
7 passed my hand across their cloth faces
8 and began to wonder how you pieced
9 all these together
10 these strips of gentle communion cotton and flannel
11 nightgowns
12 wedding organdies
13 dime-store velvets

14 how you shaped patterns square and **oblong** and round
15 positioned
16 balanced
17 then cemented them
18 with your thread
19 a steel needle
20 a thimble

21 how the thread darted in and out
22 galloping along the **frayed** edges, tucking them in
23 as you did us at night
24 oh how you stretched and turned and re-arranged
25 your michigan spring faded curtain pieces
26 my father's santa fe work shirt
27 the summer denims, the tweed of fall

28 in the evening you sat at your canvas
29 —our cracked linoleum[1] floor the drawing board
30 me lounging on your arm
31 and you staking out the plan:
32 whether to put the lilac purple of easter against the

---

1. **linoleum** a smooth, man-made floor covering with the consistency of plastic or rubber

NOTES

33 red plaid of winter-going-into-spring
34 whether to mix a yellow with blue and white and paint
35 the corpus christi[2] noon when my father held your hand
36 whether to shape a five-point star from the
37 **somber** black silk you wore to grandmother's funeral

38 you were the river current
39 carrying the roaring notes
40 forming them into pictures of a little boy reclining
41 a swallow flying
42 you were the caravan master at the reins
43 driving your thread needle **artillery** across the
44 mosaic cloth bridges
45 delivering yourself in separate testimonies

46 oh mother you **plunged** me sobbing and laughing
47 into our past
48 into the river crossing at five
49 into the spinach fields
50 into the plainview cotton rows
51 into tuberculosis wards[3]
52 into braids and muslin dresses
53 sewn hard and **taut** to withstand the thrashings of
54 twenty-five years

55 stretched out they lay
56 armed/ready/shouting/celebrating

57 knotted with love
58 the quilts sing on

"My Mother Pieced Quilts" by Teresa Palomo Acosta is reprinted with permission from the publisher of *In Other Words* (ed. Roberta Fernández) (©1994 Arte Público Press - University of Houston)

✏️ WRITE

POEM: The poem "My Mother Pieced Quilts" is told from the child's point of view. Write a poem in response to the child from the perspective of the mother.

2. **Corpus Christi** a city in southern Texas on the Gulf of Mexico
3. **tuberculosis wards** private areas of hospitals for patients with tuberculosis, a contagious infection of the lungs

Museum Indians

INFORMATIONAL TEXT
Susan Power
2002

Introduction

Winner of the 1995 Hemingway Foundation/PEN Award for Best First Fiction, Susan Power (b. 1961) has written four books, most of which deal with themes of American Indians struggling to maintain their identity and their dreams in lives outside of the reservation. Power herself is a member of the Standing Rock Tribe of the Dakotas and a descendant of Sioux Chief Mato Nupa (Two Bears). Her autobiographical essay "Museum Indians" follows Power and her Dakota-emigrant mother as they navigate the light-polluted landscape of Chicago and come face-to-face with strange markers of their Dakota ancestry in the

"... I cannot imagine my mother being afraid of anything."

1   A snake coils in my mother's dresser drawer; it is thick and black, glossy as sequins. My mother cut her hair several years ago, before I was born, but she kept one heavy braid. It is the three-foot snake I lift from its nest and handle as if it were alive.

2   "Mom, why did you cut your hair?" I ask. I am a little girl lifting a sleek black river into the light that streams through the kitchen window. Mom turns to me.

3   "It gave me headaches. Now put that away and wash your hands for lunch."

4   "You won't cut my hair, will you?" I'm sure this is a whine.

5   "No, just a little trim now and then to even your ends."

6   I return the dark snake to its nest among my mother's slips, arranging it so that its thin tail hides beneath the wide mouth sheared by scissors. My mother keeps her promise and lets my hair grow long, but I am only half of her; my thin brown braids will reach the middle of my back, and in **maturity** will look like tiny garden snakes.

7   My mother tells me stories every day: while she cleans, while she cooks, on our way to the library, standing in the checkout line at the supermarket. I like to share her stories with other people, and chatter like a monkey when I am able to **command** adult attention.

8   "She left the **reservation** when she was sixteen years old," I tell my audience. Sixteen sounds very old to me, but I always state the number because it seems **integral** to my recitation. "She had never been on a train before, or used a telephone. She left Standing Rock[1] to take a job in Chicago so she could help out the family during the war. She was petrified of all the strange people and new surroundings; she stayed in her seat all the way from McLaughlin, South Dakota, to Chicago, Illinois, and didn't move once."

9   I usually laugh after saying this, because I cannot imagine my mother being afraid of anything. She is so tall, a true Dakota[2] woman; she rises against the sun like a skyscraper, and when I draw her picture in my notebook, she takes

---

1. **Standing Rock**   a Native American Reservation located on the border of North and South Dakota
2. **Dakota**   a grouping of several Native American peoples, based on their location

NOTES

Skill:
Figurative Language

The author compares the braid to a snake with a metaphor. The metaphor helps me visualize the hair. It also helps me understand that the writer or her mother might have a connection with animals or nature.

Skill:
Figurative Language

This simile shows her mother's importance in Power's life by comparing her to a tall city building. I know it's a simile because of the word like.

Skill:
Figurative
Language

The metaphor of the shadow shows that even though she's small, Power is still connected to her mother.

Skill:
Context Clues

I'm not sure what the phrase "mount the stairs" means. It must be a verb. If stairs are involved, it must mean "to go up or down." I looked it up, and it means to "climb up." This makes sense because I can say "we climb up the stairs."

up the entire page. She talks politics and attends sit-ins, wrestles with the Chicago police and says what's on her mind.

10 I am her small shadow and witness. I am the **timid** daughter who can rage only on paper.

11 We don't have much money, but Mom takes me from one end of the city to the other on foot, on buses. I will grow up believing that Chicago belongs to me, because it was given to me by my mother. Nearly every week we tour the Historical Society, and Mom makes a point of complaining about the statue that depicts an Indian man about to kill a white woman and her children: "This is the only monument to the history of Indians in this area that you have on exhibit. It's a shame because it is completely one-sided. Children who see this will think this is what Indians are all about."

12 My mother lectures the guides and their bosses, until eventually that statue disappears.

13 Some days we haunt the Art Institute, and my mother pauses before a Picasso.

14 "He did this during his blue period," she tells me.

15 I squint at the blue man holding a blue guitar. "Was he very sad?" I ask.

16 "Yes, I think he was." My mother takes my hand and looks away from the painting. I can see a story developing behind her eyes, and I tug on her arm to release the words. She will tell me why Picasso was blue, what his thoughts were as he painted this canvas. She relates anecdotes I will never find in books, never see footnoted in a biography of the master artist. I don't even bother to check these references because I like my mother's version best.

17 When Mom is down, we go to see the mummies at the Field Museum of Natural History. The Egyptian dead sleep in the basement, most of them still shrouded in their wrappings.

18 "These were people like us," my mother whispers. She pulls me into her waist. "They had dreams and intrigues and problems with their teeth. They thought their one particular life was of the **utmost** significance. And now, just look at them." My mother never fails to brighten. "So what's the use of worrying too hard or too long? Might as well be cheerful."

19 Before we leave this place, we always visit my great-grandmother's buckskin[3] dress. We mount the stairs and walk through the museum's main hall—past the dinosaur bones all strung together, and the stuffed elephants lifting their trunks in a mute trumpet.

20 The clothed figures are disconcerting because they have no heads. I think of them as dead Indians. We reach the traditional outfits of the Sioux in the

———————————

3. **buckskin** the skin of a male deer

 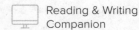

Plains Indian section, and there is the dress, as magnificent as I remembered. The yoke is completely beaded—I know the garment must be heavy to wear. My great-grandmother used blue beads as a background for the geometrical design, and I point to the azure expanse.

21 "Was this her blue period?" I ask my mother. She hushes me unexpectedly, she will not play the game. I come to understand that this is a solemn call, and we stand before the glass case as we would before a grave.

22 "I don't know how this got out of the family." Mom murmurs. I feel helpless beside her, wishing I could reach through the glass to disrobe the headless mannequin. My mother belongs in a grand buckskin dress such as this, even though her hair is now too short to braid and has been trained to curl at the edges in a saucy flip.

23 We leave our fingerprints on the glass, two sets of hands at different heights pressing against the barrier. Mom is sad to leave.

24 "I hope she knows we visit her dress," my mother says.

25 There is a little buffalo across the hall, stuffed and staring. Mom doesn't always have the heart to greet him. Some days we slip out of the museum without finding his stall.

26 "You don't belong here," Mom tells him on those rare occasions when she feels she must pay her respects. "We honor you," she continues, "because you are a creature of great **endurance** and great generosity. You provided us with so many things that helped us to survive. It makes me angry to see you like this."

27 Few things can make my mother cry; the buffalo is one of them.

28 "I am just like you," she whispers. "I don't belong here either. We should be in the Dakotas, somewhere a little bit east of the Missouri River. This crazy city is not a fit home for buffalo or Dakotas."

29 I take my mother's hand to hold her in place. I am a city child, nervous around livestock and lonely on the plains.

30 I am afraid of a sky without light pollution—I never knew there could be so many stars. I lead my mother from the museum so she will forget the sense of loss. From the marble steps we can see Lake Shore Drive spill ahead of us, and I sweep my arms to the side as if I were responsible for this view. I introduce my mother to the city she gave me. I call her home.

From *Roofwalker* by Susan Power (Minneapolis: Milkweed Editions, 2002). Copyright © 2002 by Susan Power. Reprinted with permission from Milkweed Editions. milkweed.org

First Read

Read "Museum Indians." After you read, complete the Think Questions below.

☁ **THINK QUESTIONS**

1. What made the mother scared on the train to Chicago? What does the author think about her mother's fears? Cite specific lines from the text in your answer.

2. Write two to three sentences describing the lesson that the mother takes away from the Egyptian mummies in the history museum. Is this a positive or negative lesson? Explain.

3. Why is the mother so deeply affected by the stuffed buffalo? What is her response to its presence behind glass in a museum? Include evidence from the essay in your answer.

4. Find the word **timid** in paragraph 10 of "Museum Indians." Use context clues in the surrounding sentences, as well as the sentence in which the word appears, to determine the word's meaning. Write your definition here, and identify clues that helped you figure out the meaning.

5. Use context clues to determine the meaning of **endurance** as it is used in paragraph 26 of "Museum Indians." Write your definition here, and identify clues that helped you figure out the meaning. Then check the meaning in a dictionary.

Skill:
Context Clues

Use the Checklist to analyze Context Clues in "Museum Indians." Refer to the sample student annotations about Context Clues in the text.

••• CHECKLIST FOR CONTEXT CLUES

In order to use context as a clue to infer the meaning of a word or phrase, note the following:

✓ clues about the word's part of speech

✓ clues in the surrounding text about the word's meaning

✓ signal words that cue a type of context clue, such as:

- *for example* or *for instance* to signal an example context clue
- *like, similarly,* or *just as* to signal a comparison clue
- *but, however,* or *unlike* to signal a contrast context clue

To determine the meaning of a word or phrase as it is used in a text, consider the following questions:

✓ What is the overall sentence, paragraph, or text about?

✓ How does the word function in the sentence?

✓ What clues can help me determine the word's part of speech?

✓ What text clues can help me figure out the word's definition?

✓ Are there any examples that show what the word means?

✓ What do I think the word means?

To verify the preliminary determination of the meaning of the word or phrase based on context, consider the following questions:

✓ Does the definition I inferred make sense within the context of the sentence?

✓ Which of the dictionary's definitions makes sense within the context of the sentence?

Skill:
Context Clues

Reread paragraph 2 of "Museum Indians." Then, using the Checklist on the previous page as well as the dictionary entry below, answer the multiple-choice questions.

 YOUR TURN

---

stream \\'strēm\\
noun
1. a natural body of water flowing on or under the earth
2. a steady flow of a fluid

verb
3. to flow in or as if in a stream
4. to exude a bodily fluid profusely

---

1. Which definition best matches the way the word *stream* is used in paragraph 2?

   ○ A. a natural body of water flowing on or under the earth
   ○ B. a steady flow of a fluid
   ○ C. to flow in or as if in a stream
   ○ D. to exude a bodily fluid profusely

2. Which word can we use as a context clue to help determine the correct definition of *stream*?

   ○ A. through
   ○ B. window
   ○ C. Mom
   ○ D. sleek

Please note that excerpts and passages in the StudySync® library and this workbook are intended as touchstones to generate interest in an author's work. The excerpts and passages do not substitute for the reading of entire texts, and StudySync® strongly recommends that students seek out and purchase the whole literary or informational work in order to experience it as the author intended. Links to online resellers are available in our digital library. In addition, complete works may be ordered through an authorized reseller by filling out and returning to StudySync® the order form enclosed in this workbook.

Skill:
Figurative Language

Use the Checklist to analyze Figurative Language in "Museum Indians." Refer to the sample student annotations about Figurative Language in the text.

••• CHECKLIST FOR FIGURATIVE LANGUAGE

To determine the meaning of figures of speech in a text, note the following:

✓ words that mean one thing literally and suggest something else

✓ similes, such as "strong as an ox"

✓ metaphors, such as "her eyes were stars"

✓ allusions, or indirect references, to people, texts, events, or ideas, such as

- describing a setting with the words "the place was a Garden of Eden" (biblical allusion)
- saying of a character whose snooping caused problems, "he opened a Pandora's box" (allusion to mythology)
- calling someone who likes romance "a real Romeo" (allusion to Shakespeare)

In order to interpret the meaning of a figure of speech in context, ask the following questions:

✓ Does any of the descriptive language in the text compare two seemingly unlike things?

✓ Do any descriptions include "like" or "as," indicating a simile?

✓ Is there a direct comparison that suggests a metaphor?

✓ What literary, biblical, or mythological allusions do you recognize?

✓ How does the use of this figure of speech change your understanding of the thing or person being described?

Skill:
Figurative Language

Reread paragraphs 9–10 of "Museum Indians." Then, using the Checklist on the previous page, answer the multiple-choice questions below.

⟳ YOUR TURN

1. This question has two parts. First, answer Part A. Then, answer Part B.

   Part A: The phrase "she rises against the sun like a skyscraper" is an example of a(n)—

   ○ A. simile
   ○ B. metaphor
   ○ C. extended metaphor
   ○ D. personification

   Part B: Based on the example of figurative language in Part A, the reader can infer that—

   ○ A. The mother loves her daughter.
   ○ B. The mother likes to get up early.
   ○ C. The narrator idolizes her mother.
   ○ D. The narrator and her mother argue.

Close Read

Reread "Museum Indians." As you reread, complete the Skills Focus questions below. Then use your answers and annotations from the questions to help you complete the Write activity.

⦾ SKILLS FOCUS

1. Identify evidence of the speaker's tone, or attitude, toward her mother in "Museum Indians." Explain how the speaker feels about her mother.

2. In "My Mother Pieced Quilts," the author uses descriptive details, including figurative language, to describe her mother's quilt. Identify details and examples of how the speaker in "Museum Indians" uses figurative language to describe her mother or items in the museum. What is the effect of the figurative language on the meaning or tone of the text?

3. Identify examples of the main idea or message about family in "Museum Indians." Explain what these examples suggest about family or family history.

4. In "My Mother Pieced Quilts," the author's purpose is to explore a family history, including love and loss. The speaker describes in verse how her mother would stitch pieces of fabric into quilts, each one summoning its own family history. Identify details that you can use to compare and contrast the author's purpose in "Museum Indians" with the author's purpose in "My Mother Pieced Quilts."

✏ WRITE

COMPARE AND CONTRAST: Both "My Mother Pieced Quilts" and "Museum Indians" are about love and family history. Compare and contrast the speakers in the two texts and how they interact with their mothers as well as the way they describe their family history. Include examples of figurative language in your analysis. Remember to support your ideas with evidence from the texts.

Please note that excerpts and passages in the StudySync® library and this workbook are intended as touchstones to generate interest in an author's work. The excerpts and passages do not substitute for the reading of entire texts, and StudySync® strongly recommends that students seek out and purchase the whole literary or informational work in order to experience it as the author intended. Links to online resellers are available in our digital library. In addition, complete works may be ordered through an authorized reseller by filling out and returning to StudySync® the order form enclosed in this workbook.

Reading & Writing Companion   23

The Walking Dance

FICTION
Marcela Fuentes
2017

Introduction

Marcela Fuentes is from South Texas and lives in Iowa City, Iowa, with her husband and son. She has been published in *Indiana Review*, *Storyglossia*, *Blackbird*, and *Vestal Review*. "The Walking Dance" is a short story about Gavin; his wife, Aurora; and their son, Carlos. Gavin has tried for years to fit into his wife's family, and after traveling to Laredo with his in-laws for a family funeral, he may have finally found his place. The story alternates between Gavin and Carlos's perspectives as each learns what it means to find his place within their extended family.

"... Gavin knew he'd made a mistake."

Skill:
Textual
Evidence

1   Gavin and Aurora and their children drove down from Michigan to spend Christmas in San Antonio with Aurora's family. They arrived in San Antonio on a Thursday night, and on Friday morning Aurora's uncle called from Laredo with sad news that Aurora's aunt had passed away.

2   On Sunday morning, Gavin stood in the kitchen with his son, Carlos, Aurora's brother, David, and her father, Frank, and her crazy cousin, Ricky, all of them waiting for Aurora and her mother to finish packing so they could drive to Laredo for Aunt Melchora's funeral.

3   "You guys should just ride with me," David said, gesturing to Gavin and Carlos. Gavin appreciated the invitation because even though he and Aurora made this trip every year, and even though they had been married for ten years, Gavin often still felt like an outsider in Aurora's family, especially among the men.

4   Carlos tugged at Gavin's shirt and said, "Let's go with them, Daddy! Please!" Carlos worshipped his Uncle David and Cousin Ricky. David was strong: he could still airplane eight-year-old Carlos around the room, something Gavin couldn't do anymore—and Cousin Ricky, not to be outdone, knew all the really gross things. Last Christmas he taught Carlos to say the Spanish word for eggs, *huevos*, while burping.

5   A ride with the guys sounded awesome, but Gavin had already promised Aurora he would drive her parents and the kids to Laredo. "We can't, buddy," Gavin told his son, "I promised your mom I'd drive your *abuela*[1] and Grandpa Frank." As soon as he said this, Gavin knew he'd made a mistake.

6   "Oh," Cousin Ricky teased him, "Mrs. Herrera has plans for you?"

7   "Her Highness, Princess Bossy," David said. He always called his sister that. Gavin didn't like it, but he couldn't say anything: it was between Aurora and her brother.

I know that appreciation of something like this means Gavin thinks the invitation might be a turning point in his relationship with the men in Aurora's family. He has had trouble fitting in with the family and is glad for this sign of acceptance.

---

1.   *abuela*   (Spanish) grandmother

Please note that excerpts and passages in the StudySync® library and this workbook are intended as touchstones to generate interest in an author's work. The excerpts and passages do not substitute for the reading of entire texts, and StudySync® strongly recommends that students seek out and purchase the whole literary or informational work in order to experience it as the author intended. Links to online resellers are available in our digital library. In addition, complete works may be ordered through an authorized reseller by filling out and returning to StudySync® the order form enclosed in this workbook.

Reading & Writing
Companion   25

8 "I'm being a man and taking care of my family," Gavin said. He wished Aurora understood that this is what he dealt with when he tried to fit in with the men in her family.

9 "Oh yeah?" David asked, with a sharky grin. "You want an Unknown Taco then, manly-man?"

10 "No, David," Frank, Aurora's father, said sharply. He'd been listening to them from the kitchen doorway. "No Unknown Tacos before the trip."

11 "Oh, come on, Papi," David said. "Gavin's a big boy. Aren't you, Gav?"

12 The Unknown Taco was a rite of passage[2] for men in the Herrera family. It went like this: at some point during the holidays, in front of all the other men, Aurora's father, Frank, asked one of the men if he wanted a taco. If he said yes, Frank made a taco with whatever he found in the kitchen that wasn't poisonous. The man couldn't ask what was in it, and he couldn't spit anything out: he had to finish every bite.

13 And if he said no, he was a total wuss. Forever.

14 All the men had done it. Cousin Ricky, a **massive** man who liked to say his guts were made of cast-iron, had eaten more Unknown Tacos than anyone. He swore his last taco was old coffee grounds, peanut butter, and ketchup. Aurora's brother, David, said the taco Frank gave him once was actually pickle juice and marshmallows sprinkled with eggshells. Even little Carlos had eaten an Unknown Taco. Grandpa Frank went easy on him—birthday cake and stale Halloween candy with hummus[3]—but still.

15 Gavin had been married to Aurora for ten years now, and until this day no one ever asked if he wanted an Unknown Taco. He couldn't say no.

. . .

16 Dad went to the living room, and Carlos stayed in the kitchen to watch Uncle David prepare the Unknown Taco. Uncle David made it super bad—raisins, barbeque sauce, a piece of leftover chicken enchilada, apple vinegar, pancake syrup, and a whole orange peel—and he topped it off with a half can of jalapeños. That was going to wreck his dad for sure. Back home in Michigan, when they went out to dinner his dad always had to get the extra-mild salsa while Carlos, his mom, and even his little sister, Esme, dipped into the hot no problem.

---

2. **rite of passage** an event that marks an important or transitional stage in a person's life, such as birth or transition into adulthood
3. **hummus** a dip or spread made of mashed chickpeas or beans

17 Carlos knew he should tell his dad about the jalapeños, but he worried Uncle David and Cousin Ricky wouldn't let him ride with them if he tattled, and he wanted to ride to Laredo with Uncle David and Cousin Ricky more than anything. They were the most fun people on the planet. Uncle David could do a hundred push-ups with Carlos sitting on his back counting in Spanish. Cousin Ricky was so funny. He was huge. Uncle David always said "Ricky's one chocolate bar from four hundred pounds," but he was still the best dancer in the family. On Christmas Eve, while everyone else was looking at old picture albums, he taught Carlos the Dougie and the South Dallas Swag. Best of all, Uncle David and Ricky didn't care that Carlos was a little kid—they cursed and told Carlos all kinds of stories just like he was one of the men. They made Carlos feel like he was their favorite, not Esme, who usually got all the attention because she was the baby.

18 Uncle David brought the Unknown Taco out and placed it before Dad. "Hold on," Uncle David said, then he pulled a single pink candle from his pocket, and squished it into the taco. "This is a special occasion."

19 Carlos's dad laughed nervously. "Hope you guys took it easy on me," he said.

20 Grandpa Frank stood in the doorway with arms crossed.

21 "You gonna eat your cake or what?" Cousin Ricky asked.

22 Carlos thought about his dad chugging water and his face turning the exact color of a tomato the one time he accidentally dipped into the hot salsa—he knew he should say something.

23 Carlos remained silent though, not about to miss a chance to ride with Uncle David and Cousin Ricky. Poor Dad, but too bad.

. . .

24 Aurora yelled at Gavin through the bathroom door. "It's like you woke up and decided you were gonna do dumb stuff all day!"

25 He groaned from the toilet.

26 "It doesn't even count if David makes the Unknown Taco," Aurora said. "My dad has to make it. Everyone knows that!"

27 When they finally got on the road, Gavin was too sick to drive. He sat in the back with Esme and Frank, while Aurora drove and her mother, Cookie, rode up front. Gavin slit his eyes against the bright winter sunlight, strong even

 Skill: Plot

Uncle David is challenging Gavin to eat the Unknown Taco, a tradition in Aurora's family. This is part of the conflict. Gavin wants to fit into the family.

Gavin responds to this conflict by being nervous. Grandpa Frank is crossing his arms and seems intimidating.

through the tinted windows. The air conditioning blasting directly into his face might have been the only thing keeping him from vomiting.

28   The road south of San Antonio was an empty stretch of barbed wire ranch fences, with mesquite[4] and cactus on either side of the two-lane highway. He was pretending to sleep when he heard Esme say there was a baby dinosaur crossing the highway. "Daddy! Daddy!" she yelled. "Look how small it is! Lookit, lookit, *hurry*!"

29   "Dinosaurs are extinct, honey," Gavin said, his stomach growling like a T-rex.

30   "It's an armadillo," Cookie said. Her name was actually some version of Maria where Cookie is the closest English **approximation** to the nickname, Cuquita. It's a mystery, but there it is. "Be careful, Aurora. There might be more out and I think they're endangered."

31   Aurora didn't answer her mother and she didn't slow down. Cookie the Monster, that's what Aurora called her mother when she acted bossy.

32   "Arrr-mah-di-yoh," Frank said and Esme repeated it with perfect rolling r's. Frank told her armadillos were mammals, not dinosaurs, but she refused to believe him, so Frank handed her his phone to Google it. Gavin and Aurora didn't want their daughter getting addicted to technology and never let Esme use their phones—but Gavin felt too terrible to protest.

33   "Spell it, Grandpa," Esme demanded, her small index finger poised over the touch screen. She couldn't read yet, but she knew her letters in both languages. Gavin listened to Esme and her grandpa spell it together, in Spanish. He didn't understand them very well, but Esme's attempts were bold and clear and her Grandpa Frank praised her every time.

34   She was Grandpa's girl, all right. Frank gave Esme her own set of pet names: *Esme Chula* (She's my pretty girl), *Esme Vida* (She's my life), *Esme Corazón* (She's my heart), and the only one that really annoyed Gavin, *Esme'jita* (She's my daughter). Aurora said it shouldn't bother Gavin, that Frank called all of them a pet name, even him. Which was not really true—Gavin was generic *m'ijo* since he married Aurora. Still, Frank was a better grandparent than Gavin's father, who lived an hour from Gavin and Aurora's house in Michigan but wouldn't come over unless it was someone's birthday and it didn't conflict with his bowling nights.

35   No, Gavin couldn't deny that Frank was a good guy. After all, he had tried to stop Gavin from eating the Unknown Taco. But still, *Esme'jita* bugged Gavin.

---

4. **mesquite** a type of tree native to the American Southwest that is often spiny and creates thickets

Of course Aurora didn't care: Frank still called her *mis ojos* (my eyes) and she was 36 years old.

36   "You're just jealous," Aurora teased Gavin sometimes, "because he thought of *Esme'jita* first." It was worse than that, though. It was that Gavin knew he wouldn't have thought of anything that good on his own. Only it seemed like he should have.

37   David picked that moment to roar beside them in his pickup truck, honking like a madman. He swerved into the oncoming lane, luckily free of traffic. His candy-apple red truck gleamed. As he pulled it alongside their SUV, Aurora lowered her window and rock'n'roll blared from David's truck.

38   All of a sudden Carlos popped his head and shoulders out of the truck window, with Cousin Ricky's thick forearm locked across his yellow t-shirt. Gavin watched in horror as his son hung out the truck window, shouting a challenge at his mother, "Mommy, you drive like an old lady!"

39   Grandma Cookie screamed, "Ay no! He's going to fall out!"

40   Cousin Ricky yanked Carlos back inside.

41   Aurora rolled the window up, and David's truck sped past them in a haze of black exhaust.

42   "Ricky, you're dead!" Aurora yelled. The SUV lunged after the truck like someone gave it a good kick, and the Unknown Taco leapt into Gavin's chest.

43   Cookie demanded Frank call David, and Frank said something sharp to Aurora in Spanish. Gavin didn't know what, but he knew what her name sounded like when her dad was angry. Aurora kept her foot on the floor and the SUV surged until they were beside David's red truck.

44   "Don't kill the dinosaur, Mommy!" Esme wailed. "Watch out for the dinosaur!" Sure enough, there was another ugly gray armadillo, smack in the middle of the road.

45   Aurora and David both swerved around it, spraying gravel into the ditches along the highway. David honked hard and she honked back, but let off the gas. David pulled ahead, swerved into the right lane, and sped away.

46   "You did it, Mommy," Esme gasped. "You saved the baby dinosaur."

47   "'Course I did, sweetheart," Aurora said. "I'm a professional." She sounded totally calm, as if she hadn't just been scaring them all into fits.

NOTES

48 There was a fantastic blue horizon in front of Gavin, sweet with high white cloud streaks and David's red truck was already disappearing over the next hill. Gavin couldn't help himself. He vomited.

. . .

49 Coming into Laredo from San Antonio was like approaching a fortress. A military-style checkpoint with armed border patrol agents and German Shepherd police dogs, just to get into the city. Carlos watched from the passenger window of Uncle David's truck while the K-9 patrol sniffed vehicles headed north. Southbound, there were lots of trucks with Minnesota and Wisconsin and even Michigan license plates, all of them piled high with toys and bicycles and skateboards and kitchen appliances and furniture. Sometimes a tarp flapped over it all, other times everything was just tied together with rope. The trucks looked like overflowing shopping carts waiting in line at the checkout.

50 "What's all that?" Carlos asked.

51 "Christmas presents," Uncle David said. "Guys come work in the states and have families in Mexico. So, you know. Daddy's bringing home the bacon."

52 "But like a year's worth of bacon," Ricky added.

53 Carlos could not imagine his dad being away for an entire year, or his dad hauling a big load of gifts across the whole country. Just to visit San Antonio for Christmas, Mom had to give their dog, Chewbacca, knock-out pills and kennel him the whole time, or else Dad complained about bringing him.

54 Yes, Carlos decided, Laredo was definitely a weird city.

55 When they arrived at the funeral home, Carlos noticed a half dozen helicopters parked across the street in a brushy dirt lot behind a barbed wire fence. The compound looked like a circus, with tents and Quonset huts, and men in fatigues, but Uncle David and Ricky didn't find the helicopters unusual. When Carlos pointed them out, Ricky just shrugged and said, "We're on the border." Carlos mulled this over, but it didn't make sense to him. His mom had taken him to Windsor, across the Canadian border from Detroit. There was just a city, then a toll booth, and a cool big tunnel, and then even though they were in Canada, it looked the same.

56 Uncle David and Ricky started to talk about their Aunt Bea. They called her the witch. She was their aunt, which meant she was Carlos's aunt, too. She was supposed to be here at the funeral home, along with at least a hundred other relatives he didn't know.

57 "She's literally a witch?" Carlos asked. His mom was always telling him there's a big difference between literally and figuratively. Literally was the truth; the actual thing. Figuratively was just how you feel, so Carlos asked again, "Like for real a witch?"

58 "She's evil," Uncle David said.

59 "Watch it," Uncle Ricky hissed, looking around.

60 "So it's true?" Carlos persisted.

61 "Don't say that too loud," Uncle David said. "She's crazy."

62 "Yeah," Ricky said. "The last time I saw Aunt Bea was at a family reunion a couple years back. She can't swim, but she was wading into the ocean off of South Padre Island."

63 Uncle David laughed. "Poor Tío just stood there saying, 'C'mon, Beatríz, get in the car already.'"

64 This didn't sound very witchy to Carlos, but it was kind of creepy. Sometimes his mom and dad took Esme and him out to Lake Superior, which was the most water he could imagine in one place. "What if she drowned?" Carlos asked.

65 "Oh Buddy, she wasn't gonna," Uncle David assured him. "She was just being dramatic."

66 "Yeah, no such luck," Ricky said. "*Mírala*, there she is."

67 Ricky pointed with his lips—it looked like a duck-face—toward the steps of the funeral home at an elderly woman wearing a slash of bright red lipstick and a cheetah-print dress: Aunt Bea. "Stay away from her," Ricky told Carlos. "I remember one time we were playing hide and seek, me and David found some *bruja* stuff in the crawl space under the house." Ricky wrinkled his nose. "A rotting watermelon with little ribbons and charms and pins stuck into the rind."

68 "Man, you're scaring him," said Uncle David.

69 "I'm not scared," Carlos countered. He was a little scared, but he had to hear it. Carlos wished his family could move to Texas and live near Mom's family. His family visited from Michigan every Christmas, but it was not enough. The Herreras lived and breathed mysteries. Grandma Cookie was always praying over him with a raw egg in case of the evil eye, and if Carlos ever had a bad

dream, Grandpa Frank sprinkled holy water under the bed to ward off spirits. And when his uncles told these stories, they meant them.

70   "Oh, and that blood," Ricky was saying. "I still think that was chicken blood inside that watermelon. Remember?"

71   "I dunno," said Uncle David, "but she and Tío got in a big fight about it. He started hollering and throwing all her things in the yard. Even the sewing machine."

72   "What nonsense are you telling him?"

73   It was Carlos's Mom, thank goodness. Dad was right behind her. Right away, Carlos could tell his dad was in a bad mood. But still, he was so relieved to see them that he forgot and said, "Hey, Mommy," just like little Esme would.

74   "I better never catch you hanging out of a moving vehicle again," Mom said, hugging him hard. Carlos couldn't see Mom's eyes behind the huge pink sunglasses she was wearing, but she didn't seem too mad, and she never stayed mad for too long anyway. Grandpa Frank said it was because she has a ticklish temper. Even when she got mad, she saw something funny in it. Still, Carlos knew there was no way she would ever let him ride with Uncle David again. He wasn't sorry, though. It had been worth it.

75   Mom was on speaker phone with Grandma Cookie, even though they were in the same parking lot. Grandma said she was taking Esme to the bathroom, and then, still on the phone, Grandma started greeting people inside the funeral home.

76   Mom looked at Carlos. "Hey, you call that lady *Tía* Bea when you say hello. She's your aunt."

77   "Only by marriage," Grandma Cookie said over the phone, then she hung up.

78   "Really?" Dad blurted out.

79   "Stop being such a baby," Mom told him. "She wasn't talking about you."

80   "She said that right in front of me."

81   "No she didn't. Anyway, you barfed in the car."

82   "Whatsamatter, a little sick today, Goldilocks?" Ricky said, patting Dad on the belly like a little baby.

83   Dad ignored Ricky. Mom shook her head.

84 "By the way David, don't let Mom find you, for real. She's so mad at you," Mom said in a bratty tone, just like Esme's when she tattled on Carlos. "See you guys inside."

85 Mom wiggled her fingers at them and strolled off. It was funny when she acted like a sister more than a mom. Carlos had even seen her give Uncle David noogies. That was one of the magic things that happened when they visited Texas.

86 Dad hung his arms over the fence and spit. He looked pale. But he squinted at the helicopters. Carlos was glad someone else noticed them. "Are those Black Hawks?" Dad asked.

87 "They can't be," Ricky said. "Black Hawks would be at a military base. That's not a base."

88 "Actually, yes, they are," said Uncle David. "Those are UH-60s. I should know. Those guys are Border Patrol."

89 "Border Patrol is para-military," Ricky said. "*Para*. That means not really."

90 "What do you know about it?" Uncle David asked. "I'm out there every day."

91 "You've never been in a helicopter in your life," Ricky said.

92 "That's what you think," Uncle David said. "I can't discuss my work."

93 "Whatever," Ricky said.

94 "Man, shut up, you sell air conditioners for a living."

95 They kept bickering and Carlos turned back to look for Tía Bea, who was still on the steps, her pouchy eyes and skin looking fragile, papery, like she was wearing too much powder. Maybe she was just very old. She was spooky. Carlos had no trouble at all imagining her stalking into the Gulf of Mexico, or witch-cursing someone.

96 "Don't stare at her," Uncle David whispered. "She can give the evil eye at twenty paces."

97 She saw them watching her and called across the parking lot in a creaky voice, "Hi, *m'ijos*."

98 "Hey, Aunt Bea," Uncle David and Ricky shouted, fake-smiling.

• • •

99   The chapel service was set for 7 p.m., and Aurora's relatives packed the lobby. Everyone spoke in quiet voices, but there were so many people talking that the air hummed. To Gavin it felt oddly festive. People hugged and laughed. They kissed their hands and pressed them to the giant double photograph on the mantle of the fake fireplace. Half of the picture was a black and white of a young brunette, very nineteen-fifties Elizabeth Taylor, and the other half was a digital color photo of an old woman in a lavender Easter dress, her hair a cropped white nimbus. Aurora had coached Gavin on this. The woman was—had been—Cookie's oldest sister, Melchora.

100 *Melchora, Melchora, rhymes with Aurora.* There was something in the eyes of the black and white girl that he recognized . . . and in the photograph of the old woman there was also an approximation of his wife, which he found disquieting. Gavin looked around. Somewhere in this human traffic jam of a lobby was a widower whom Gavin had never met and whose name he didn't know.

101 He found Esme and Aurora outside the back of the building, on a patio that faced the interstate. Esme wound herself around the railings of the stairs. Grandma Cookie had dressed her in a navy blue herringbone jumper and a new pair of gold shoes, the same color Cookie herself was wearing. All the better to **accentuate** Esme's position as the only granddaughter, Gavin guessed. "Are we ready to go in?" he asked Aurora.

102 Aurora shrugged. It was dark out and she'd taken off her sunglasses. She was backlit by the streetlights and her face was hazy, muted by the shadows, and her eyes were dark. She was older than her aunt had been in the black and white photo, but Gavin could see her in the progression between the photographs, everything mapped out and inevitable, just the eyes looking out at him until they stopped seeing altogether. There was a guy in there with a dead wife, and Gavin didn't even know who he was. Not knowing that guy scared him so much. If something happened to Aurora, he'd be swallowed up by her mammoth family, totally invisible. Barely anyone would know him.

103 Gavin hugged Aurora, and she let him, but gave him a little pinch just so he'd know he was still in the dog house for vomiting in the car. "How's your tummy?" she asked him.

104 "Better," he said. The scary feeling shrank to something small and ridiculous. But it wasn't all the way gone. *Melchora, Melchora, rhymes with Aurora.*

105 It ended up that there wasn't a lot of praying during the chapel service. People came up to the podium beside the casket and told stories about Melchora. A young kid with a ponytail, who everybody called Ponchi, spent the rest of the service Spanish rapping over songs with heavy, thumping bass.

106 "¡Ayla!" Grandpa Frank said. "What is this noise?"

107 "Ponchi lives in Los Angeles," Aurora whispered to Gavin behind her hand. "He's a recording artist."

108 "I like it," said Carlos, grooving in his seat.

109 "Ponchi," said Ricky, rolling his eyes. "Ever since he was a game show contestant on *Univisión* last year, he thinks he's the second coming of Pitbull."

110 "I wrote this one for my grandmother," Ponchi said from beside the casket. "This is '*Abuela Mella*.'"

111 People were shifting, getting out of their seats and soon there were clumps of dancers moving in a slow circle around the room in a **leisurely** *cumbia*. Gavin knew the *cumbia* pretty well, because Aurora was a fan of the late Tejano Queen, Selena. Aurora would holler "That's my jam!" and make Gavin dance around the living room with her. She called it the walking dance. You could be doing anything—cleaning the house, talking on the phone, carrying groceries—and as long as you made the *cumbia* circle, you were doing it right. It was the only dance Gavin was good at because he could walk around doing his own freestyle moves.

112 He watched the line of dancers shift and weave slowly, undulating like a lazy snake among the pews. The relatives were chatting and dancing, then they were weeping and dancing. He didn't know what that Ponchi kid was saying, but it was making some of them smile, some of them hold each other, some of them shake their heads. Cookie and Frank got up, taking Carlos with them. There were so many dancers. Teenage girls in clacky shoes pulled their baby cousins along; in fact, there was Esme, who had slipped off without asking, being swung from spot to spot by two girls. A clutch of burly, tattooed men, one of them with a tiny baby in the beefy crook of an elbow, shuffled along. "Michelangelo," Aurora murmured. "That's the new baby, Michelangelo." He looked like a small, wide-eyed potato. Old men dressed like cowboys. Young men dressed like cowboys, in denim shirts and leather vests; powdered old women, and gyrating young women, all with glittering earrings and shiny hair, danced. Everyone danced. There was the funeral home director, solemn faced and dancing alone, taking his turn around the room. Two boys behind him made faces at his back, but he didn't see them.

113 Cousin Ricky slipped into the groove of dancers, taking the hand of a woman Gavin didn't know. On the dance floor Ricky was mesmerizing, practically a work of art: a giant, hairy mammoth that somehow, even sweating through his Hawaiian shirt, in defiance of all laws of physics and the universe, achieved beauty—that's how deeply he felt the music. He did a slow strut, spun his

Please note that excerpts and passages in the StudySync® library and this workbook are intended as touchstones to generate interest in an author's work. The excerpts and passages do not substitute for the reading of entire texts, and StudySync® strongly recommends that students seek out and purchase the whole literary or informational work in order to experience it as the author intended. Links to online resellers are available in our digital library. In addition, complete works may be ordered through an authorized reseller by filling out and returning to StudySync® the order form enclosed in this workbook.

Reading & Writing Companion   **35**

partner in place, and then again so she revolved around him. Dancers cat-called Ricky and his partner, spurring them on to more twirls.

114   Aurora stood up, dropping her scarf on the pew, and held out her hand to her brother. "C'mon, Davykins," she said. "Dance with me."

115   "Davykins," Gavin snorted, feeling left out. This was the kind of song he could actually dance to. How could she pick David? Everything that had gone wrong today was David's fault! But, no, of course it didn't matter—even if he was thirty years old, David was Aurora's baby brother, and Gavin was just her husband.

116   "¡Vámonos!" David said. He grabbed Gavin's wife by the hand and they hustled into the line. David shook disco fists while Aurora flung her arms out in an exaggerated sprinkler. They shook along the circuit of dancers.

117   "C'mon fool, get up!" Cousin Ricky yelled as he swooped by and lifted Gavin by the blazer. "You're gonna get labeled the non-dancing white guy."

118   "Don't be that guy," Cousin Ricky's dance partner said.

119   Gavin joined them. Being in the mix was **disorienting**, and Gavin shuffled, trying to sway on beat and settling into a pace that wouldn't bump the old lady in front of him and avoided the aggressive spins Cousin Ricky and his partner were doing behind him. It was hard. Gavin couldn't tell if this was the longest song in the history of songs, or more than one song. The tropical beat kept grinding out of the audio mixer: *chuk-chukka-chuk, chuk-chukka-chuk.*

120   Gavin glanced around. The crowd had swallowed Cousin Ricky, and in his place, a short guy with a dirty turkey feather stuck in the hatband of his black Stetson was dancing alone. Suddenly, Carlos intercepted Gavin at the turn near the front of the chapel, where that Ponchi kid was still belting out lyrics.

121   "Daddy," Carlos gasped, with tears in his eyes. "Daddy, that lady is dead! I saw her. She's really dead."

122   "I know, son." He steered Carlos out of the stream of dancers, into an empty pew. "I know, buddy."

123   Gavin didn't know what else to say. Carlos's sobs were hot and damp against his shirt. Across the room, Esme rode on Grandpa Frank's shoulders, squinting with laughter. She had got both hands clamped in Frank's hair, which must have hurt, but Frank kept dancing anyway, one hand holding her steady. Gavin felt dizzy. He couldn't see Aurora anywhere, and everything was

Skill:
Plot

Cousin Ricky is yelling at Gavin for not dancing. This scene shows that Gavin is still struggling to fit in with the family.

Gavin responds by deciding to join even though the place is crowded and he's uncomfortable. He really wants to be part of the family and feel accepted by Aurora's brothers. He's kind of taking a risk here.

closing over him: his son's grief, the never-ending music, all these strangers moving and moving and moving.

124   "What's the matter?" Cookie demanded. She had a special sense: when it came to her grandkids she could smell trouble even in a room full of dancing mourners.

125   "Grandma," Carlos said. "What if you die?"

126   "When I do, you throw me a big party too. I'm putting you in charge. You pick the music."

127   "No! I don't want to be in charge. I want you to be alive!"

128   Carlos shoved his face into her midsection, howling in a way he hadn't since he was younger. Cookie rocked him, clutching him tight and burying her hand in Carlos's wavy hair. She made a noise Gavin could not describe, something like *yooo, yooo, yooo*—soft, wordless crooning, pitched so low Gavin could hear it even through the din.

129   Cookie was a tiny woman, not much bigger than Carlos. She swayed with the effort to hold on to him. She'd been crying, but she was also flushed with the exertion of dancing.

130   That's her sister over there dead, Gavin thought, but she was riding out Carlos's sobs like he was the only thing that mattered in the entire world. Somehow, it was just the three of them together inside the pulsing bass.

131   Gavin didn't know how to talk to his son about death any more than he could dream up sweet nicknames for his daughter. He was not quick-witted like Frank, nor was he cool like David or Ricky. But he could do the walking dance. He remembered what Aurora had told him. "It's a dance you can do carrying a bag of groceries." It was a dance he could do, Gavin decided, even carrying a crying kid.

132   He lifted Carlos out of Cookie's arms. This kiddo was heavy, but Gavin could tough it out for at least one lap around the chapel with his mother-in-law.

133   "Come on," Gavin said, holding a hand out to Cookie. "Let's get back out there."

134   "That's right." Cookie pressed her fist to her eyes, hard. "That's right. Let's go."

Marcela Fuentes is a graduate of the Iowa Writers' Workshop. She's lived all over the United States but most often writes about her home state, Texas.

First Read

Read "The Walking Dance." After you read, complete the Think Questions below.

☁ THINK QUESTIONS

1. Why does Gavin think it is difficult being around Aurora's family? Cite specific evidence from the text to support your answer.

2. What is Carlos's opinion of his uncle David and Cousin Ricky? How do his opinions affect his decisions and behavior? Cite specific evidence from the text to support your answer.

3. Refer to details in the text to explain why Uncle David and Cousin Ricky call Tía Bea a witch, or *bruja*.

4. Find the word **approximation** in paragraph 30 of "The Walking Dance." Use context clues in the surrounding sentences, as well as the sentence in which the word appears, to determine the word's meaning. Write your definition here and identify clues that helped you figure out the meaning.

5. Use context clues to determine the meaning of **leisurely** as it is used in paragraph 111 of "The Walking Dance." Write your definition here and identify clues that helped you figure out the meaning. Then check the meaning in a dictionary.

PLOT

Skill:
Plot

Use the Checklist to analyze Plot in "The Walking Dance." Refer to the sample student annotations about Plot in the text.

••• CHECKLIST FOR PLOT

In order to identify particular elements of a story or drama, note the following:

✓ setting details

✓ character details, including their thoughts, actions, and descriptions

✓ notable incidents or events in the plot

✓ characters or setting details that may have caused an event to occur

✓ the central conflict and the characters who are involved

✓ dialogue between or among characters

✓ instances when setting interferes with a character's motivations

To analyze how particular elements of a story or drama interact, consider the following questions:

✓ How do the events of the plot unfold in the story?

✓ How do characters respond or change as the plot advances?

✓ How does the setting shape the characters or the plot?

✓ How does a particular scene in the story contribute to development of the plot?

Please note that excerpts and passages in the StudySync® library and this workbook are intended as touchstones to generate interest in an author's work. The excerpts and passages do not substitute for the reading of entire texts, and StudySync® strongly recommends that students seek out and purchase the whole literary or informational work in order to experience it as the author intended. Links to online resellers are available in our digital library. In addition, complete works may be ordered through an authorized reseller by filling out and returning to StudySync® the order form enclosed in this workbook.

Reading & Writing Companion   **39**

PLOT

Skill: Plot

Reread paragraphs 24–27 of "The Walking Dance." Then, using the Checklist on the previous page, answer the multiple-choice questions below.

⟳ YOUR TURN

1. How does Aurora's reaction in paragraph 24 relate to the conflict of the story?

   ○ A. It helps to develop the arguing between Aurora and Gavin as the main conflict of the story.
   ○ B. It shows that Gavin's first attempt to fit in with Aurora's family has been unsuccessful.
   ○ C. It builds interest in the story because Aurora is angry that Gavin could not tolerate the Unknown Taco.
   ○ D. It emphasizes that Gavin does not fit in with the family because he makes poor decisions.

2. How is Aurora's statement in paragraph 26 important to the plot?

   ○ A. It suggests that Gavin will never be accepted by Aurora's family.
   ○ B. It foreshadows that Gavin will confront Aurora's brother for tricking him into eating the Unknown Taco.
   ○ C. It reveals that Gavin is still an outsider in Aurora's family because the Unknown Taco he ate didn't count.
   ○ D. It suggests that Aurora and Gavin will continue fighting because Gavin is upset he was tricked by Aurora's brother.

Skill:
Textual Evidence

Use the Checklist to analyze Textual Evidence in "The Walking Dance." Refer to the sample student annotations about Textual Evidence in the text.

••• CHECKLIST FOR TEXTUAL EVIDENCE

In order to support an analysis by citing textual evidence that is explicitly stated in the text, do the following:

- ✓ read the text closely and critically

- ✓ identify what the text says explicitly

- ✓ find the most relevant textual evidence that supports your analysis

- ✓ consider why an author explicitly states specific details and information

- ✓ cite the specific words, phrases, sentences, paragraphs, or images from the text that support your analysis

In order to interpret implicit meanings in a text by making inferences, do the following:

- ✓ combine information directly stated in the text with your own knowledge, experiences, and observations

- ✓ cite the specific words, phrases, sentences, paragraphs, or images from the text that support this inference

In order to cite textual evidence to support an analysis of what the text says explicitly as well as inferences drawn from the text, consider the following questions:

- ✓ Have I read the text closely and critically?

- ✓ What inferences am I making about the text? What textual evidence am I using to support these inferences?

- ✓ Am I quoting the evidence from the text correctly?

- ✓ Does my textual evidence logically relate to my analysis?

- ✓ Have I cited several pieces of textual evidence?

Skill:
Textual Evidence

Reread paragraphs 114–119 of "The Walking Dance." Then, using the Checklist on the previous page, answer the multiple-choice questions below.

⟳ YOUR TURN

1. Which part of the passage provides the clearest evidence that Gavin feels he cannot compete with Aurora's family for her attention?

   ○ A. "C'mon, Davykins," she said. "Dance with me."

   ○ B. But, no, of course it didn't matter—even if he was thirty years old, David was Aurora's baby brother, and Gavin was just her husband.

   ○ C. David shook disco fists while Aurora flung her arms out in an exaggerated sprinkler.

   ○ D. Gavin couldn't tell if this was the longest song in the history of songs, or more than one song.

2. Cousin Ricky's words and actions in paragraph 117 help the reader infer that—

   ○ A. he thinks Gavin is rude and is behaving foolishly.

   ○ B. he wants Gavin to get out on the floor so he can make fun of Gavin.

   ○ C. he wants to include Gavin in the family's activities.

   ○ D. he thinks Gavin does not know how to dance.

3. Which part of the passage provides the best evidence to support the inference that Gavin is uncomfortable on the dance floor?

   ○ A. This was the kind of song he could actually dance to.

   ○ B. "Don't be that guy," Cousin Ricky's dance partner said.

   ○ C. Gavin shuffled, trying to sway on beat and settling into a pace that wouldn't bump the old lady in front of him.

   ○ D. The tropical beat kept grinding out of the audio mixer: *chuk-chukka-chuk, chuk-chukka-chuk.*

Close Read

Reread "The Walking Dance." As you reread, complete the Skills Focus questions below. Then use your answers and annotations from the questions to help you complete the Write activity.

◎ SKILLS FOCUS

1. Identify and highlight notable conflicts or incidents in the plot. Explain why they are important to the plot or how they affect the characters.

2. Identify and highlight the turning point and resolution. Explain how those events impact the characters and contribute to the meaning of the story.

3. Identify and highlight two or three places where a character's actions or dialogue have a direct impact on the plot. Explain how the plot is affected by that character's actions or dialogue.

4. Identify an important message or idea expressed in the story. Highlight examples of this message in the story, and explain how each example demonstrates that idea.

5. Explain what the characters in this story learn from their experiences with love and loss. Highlight examples of characters responding to loss or love, and write a note about how those experiences affect the characters.

✏ WRITE

LITERARY ANALYSIS: How does Marcela Fuentes use plot elements and events such as conflict, turning action, and resolution to convey the theme of this story? Write a short response in which you specify one theme and explain how those plot elements help to convey it. Use several pieces of textual evidence to support your response.

Please note that excerpts and passages in the StudySync® library and this workbook are intended as touchstones to generate interest in an author's work. The excerpts and passages do not substitute for the reading of entire texts, and StudySync® strongly recommends that students seek out and purchase the whole literary or informational work in order to experience it as the author intended. Links to online resellers are available in our digital library. In addition, complete works may be ordered through an authorized reseller by filling out and returning to StudySync® the order form enclosed in this workbook.

Reading & Writing Companion   **43**

Second Estrangement

POETRY
Aracelis Girmay
2014

Introduction

Aracelis Girmay (b. 1977) has authored three award-winning collections of poetry, including *Kingdom Animalia*, a finalist for the prestigious National Book Critics Circle award. Her poems are often brief and revelatory, commonly exploring themes of the African diaspora in its manifold forms in a voice at once distinct and beautiful. "Second Estrangement" appears in Girmay's book *The Black Maria*.

"Please raise your hand, whomever else of you has been a child, / lost . . ."

1 Please raise your hand,
2 whomever else of you
3 has been a child,
4 lost, in a market
5 or a mall, without
6 knowing it at first, following
7 a stranger, **accidentally**
8 thinking he is yours,
9 your family or parent, even
10 grabbing for his hands,
11 even calling the word
12 you said then for "Father,"
13 only to see the face
14 look strangely down, **utterly**
15 foreign, utterly not the one
16 who loves you, you
17 who are a bird suddenly
18 **stunned** by the glass **partitions**
19 of rooms.
20   How far
21 the world you knew, & tall,
22 & filled, finally, with strangers.

 Skill:
Poetic Elements
and Structure

NOTES

The speaker tries to get me to remember how it feels to be a child by asking me to raise my hand. It feels like I'm a kid being talked to.

It's open verse because there's no rhyme or rhythm. The lines are also short and break apart the sentence. This makes me feel weird, like I don't know what's coming next. For each line, I see myself as a kid trying to catch up with my dad!

Aracelis Girmay, "Second Estrangement" from *The Black Maria*. Copyright ©2016 Aracelis Girmay. Reprinted with the permission of The Permissions Company, Inc. on behalf of BOA Editions Ltd., www.boaeditions.org.

First Read

Read "Second Estrangement." After you read, complete the Think Questions below.

 THINK QUESTIONS

1. What are the settings mentioned in the poem? Where else could such a situation occur? Cite evidence from the text in support of your answer.

2. What does the writer mean when the speaker calls out the word she "said then for 'Father'"? Cite evidence from the text in support of your answer.

3. To what action does the speaker compare a bird "stunned by the glass partitions"? Cite evidence from the text in support of your answer.

4. What is the meaning of the word **estrangement** as it is used in the text? Write your best definition here, along with a brief explanation of the context clues that helped you arrive at the definition.

5. Based on context clues, what do you think the word **utterly** means? Write your best definition of *utterly* here and explain how you figured it out.

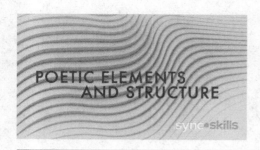

Skill:
Poetic Elements and Structure

Use the Checklist to analyze Poetic Elements and Structure in "Second Estrangement." Refer to the sample student annotations about Poetic Elements and Structure in the text.

••• CHECKLIST FOR POETIC ELEMENTS AND STRUCTURE

In order to identify poetic elements and structure, note the following:

- ✓ the form and overall structure of the poem

- ✓ the rhyme, rhythm, and meter, if present

- ✓ lines and stanzas in the poem that suggest its meaning

- ✓ ways that the poem's form or structure connects to the poem's meaning

To analyze how a poem's form or structure contributes to its meaning, consider the following questions:

- ✓ What poetic form does the poet use? What is the structure?

- ✓ How do the lines and stanzas and their lengths affect the meaning?

- ✓ How do the form and the structure contribute to the poem's meaning?

Please note that excerpts and passages in the StudySync® library and this workbook are intended as touchstones to generate interest in an author's work. The excerpts and passages do not substitute for the reading of entire texts, and StudySync® strongly recommends that students seek out and purchase the whole literary or informational work in order to experience it as the author intended. Links to online resellers are available in our digital library. In addition, complete works may be ordered through an authorized reseller by filling out and returning to StudySync® the order form enclosed in this workbook.

Reading & Writing
Companion   47

Skill:
Poetic Elements and Structure

Reread lines 20–22 of "Second Estrangement." Then, using the Checklist on the previous page, answer the multiple-choice questions below.

↻ YOUR TURN

1. The first line contains only two words, "How far." What is the effect of this two-word line?

   - ○ A. This is not an important line.
   - ○ B. These words are mirroring the meaning of the poem.
   - ○ C. There was not enough room on the previous line.
   - ○ D. The poet was not very careful when writing.

2. Lines 20–22 are important because they—

   - ○ A. include the punctuation "&," which represents being connected to family.
   - ○ B. convey the central idea that this is an important moment in a child's life.
   - ○ C. help to establish the regular rhyme scheme and meter of this poem.
   - ○ D. show that the child will never find her father again.

Close Read

Reread "Second Estrangement." As you reread, complete the Skills Focus questions below. Then use your answers and annotations from the questions to help you complete the Write activity.

◎ SKILLS FOCUS

1. The author repeats the words *you* and *your* throughout the poem. What effect does this have on the reader? Explain how this influences the message of the poem.

2. Reread lines 4–8. How do the lines' length and structure affect the reader? How do their length and structure help to convey their meaning?

3. Identify details in the last three lines that help to develop the theme in the poem. Explain how these details accomplish this.

4. The author of "Second Estrangement" wrote a series of poems with *estrangement* in the title that focus on separation and loss. How does this poem explore the concept of loss? How does the structure of the poem help contribute to the sense of estrangement?

✏ WRITE

LITERARY ANALYSIS: What do you think is the deeper meaning or message of the poem "Second Estrangement"? How does the poet's use of poetic structure, such as open form and line length, contribute to the poem's deeper meaning? Write a response to this question, using evidence from the poem to support your response.

Please note that excerpts and passages in the StudySync® library and this workbook are intended as touchstones to generate interest in an author's work. The excerpts and passages do not substitute for the reading of entire texts, and StudySync® strongly recommends that students seek out and purchase the whole literary or informational work in order to experience it as the author intended. Links to online resellers are available in our digital library. In addition, complete works may be ordered through an authorized reseller by filling out and returning to StudySync® the order form enclosed in this workbook.

Reading & Writing Companion   49

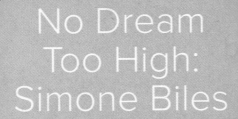

No Dream Too High: Simone Biles

INFORMATIONAL TEXT
Alex Shultz
2017

Introduction

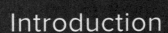

Born in 1997, American gymnast Simone Biles overcame a difficult childhood—from the absence of her biological parents to her diminutive, 4-foot-8 frame—to become the most decorated athlete in the history of her sport. In this profile, author Alex Shultz explores the pressures of great expectations and the many sacrifices Biles, a hero to millions, has made on the road to glory. Shultz's profile also reveals how Biles has battled her own demons and the outrage of certain people who remain hostile to the success of an African American woman in a

"'Simone's just in her own league. Whoever gets second place, that's the winner.'"

1   The floor routine[1] was all that stood between Simone Biles and her first all-around world championship. Biles smiled from ear to ear, revealing her braces. She was sixteen years old. She sprinted across the mat, effortlessly completing two somersaults and two twists in one leap, a double-double in gymnastics terms. She danced her way to another corner, tilted her chin up, and launched into something no one had ever seen before this event. Biles soared through the air, flipped twice, and landed on her feet, face-forward. The announcers on NBC described it as "a double layout with a half" twist. The crowd knew it as something else: The Biles, a maneuver so exceptional that it was named after her. It was her first major international competition, and Biles had crushed the rest of the field, largely because of a move she had created.

 NOTES

"THE BILES"

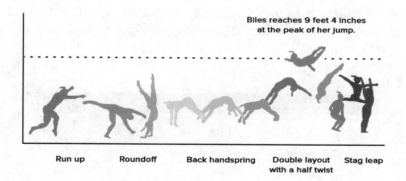

Biles reaches 9 feet 4 inches at the peak of her jump.

Run up   Roundoff   Back handspring   Double layout with a half twist   Stag leap

 Skill: Central or Main Idea

2   The 2013 world championships marked Simone Biles's arrival on the **elite** gymnastics scene. Four years later, her accolades include three all-around world championships, and four gold medals and one bronze at the 2016 Olympics. As Olympics teammate Aly Raisman told the *New Yorker*, "Simone's just in her own league. Whoever gets second place, that's the winner." Biles

These details suggest the central idea is Biles is an amazing, one-of-a-kind athlete. She's won many awards and is "in her own league."

1. **floor routine** an event in gymnastics competition in which the gymnasts perform various maneuvers on a special spring-loaded floor

is a once-in-a-generation athlete with limitless talent and a strong dedication to her sport. She is a gymnast like no other.

Beginnings

3 Were it not for some bad weather, Simone Biles might never have become a gymnast at all. When she was six years old, her daycare redirected an outdoor field trip to a gymnastics studio because of rain. Biles told ESPN that at the time she was a "very crazy, very hyper and energetic" girl capable of mimicking the more difficult moves of some of the older girls at the studio. This attracted the attention of the coaches in attendance. Soon after, she enrolled at Bannon's Gymnastix in Houston.

4 Like anyone starting out at a new sport, Biles struggled with the **fundamentals.** In a profile of Biles for Buzzfeed, Dvora Meyers wrote, "She isn't naturally flexible and couldn't find the right shapes on her leaps and jumps. She also didn't know how to control her immense power, often bounding up and back several feet after landing tumbling passes. And on bars—the most technical event in the women's repertoire[2]—she lacked **finesse."** By the time Biles was 16, though, she was a blossoming star.

5 During the years Biles was developing into an elite athlete, the sport of gymnastics was also changing. In the past, gymnastics was more about finesse than power, and the various competitions within it were graded on a 10-point scale. Many times, the winner of an event would score a perfect 10. That changed in 2006, when the points system split into two: an **execution** score and a difficulty score. The execution score is still out of 10 points and is awarded based on how well a gymnast performs a routine. The difficulty score awards additional points based on the **rigor** of the skills attempted during the routine.

2016 OLYMPICS — WOMEN'S GYMNASTICS ALL-AROUND FINAL — VAULT				
ATHLETE	COUNTRY	DIFFICULTY SCORE (VAULT)	EXECUTION SCORE (VAULT)	FINAL SCORE (VAULT)
Simone Biles	United States	6.300	9.566	15.866
Aly Raisman	United States	6.300	9.333	15.633
Aliya Mustafina	Russia	5.800	9.400	15.200

2. **repertoire** one's collection of skills or things one can do

6   The difficulty score aided Biles because the routines she performs are more challenging than what other gymnasts attempt. For example, prior to her floor routine at the all-around world championships in 2013, she was actually in second place, behind another American competitor, Kyla Ross. Biles's floor program was more difficult than Ross's, though. When Biles finished it with no errors she easily won the title.

7   Part of Biles's natural talent also stems from her height or lack thereof. In some sports, height is an advantage, but gymnasts benefit from being shorter. From 2000–2012, the four all-around gold medal winners at the Olympics were between 5-foot and 5-foot-3. While that might seem short for most athletes, Biles stands at just 4 feet 8 inches. Her height bothered her as a child. As she told *Women's Health*, "it was kind of a struggle being small since everyone would make fun of you," but she's glad she can show others that they can be "short or tall" and become the best.

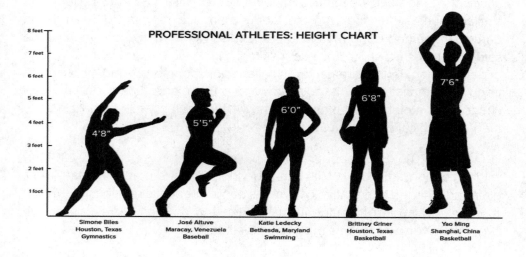

PROFESSIONAL ATHLETES: HEIGHT CHART

	Height
Simone Biles Houston, Texas Gymnastics	4'8"
José Altuve Maracay, Venezuela Baseball	5'5"
Katie Ledecky Bethesda, Maryland Swimming	6'0"
Brittney Griner Houston, Texas Basketball	6'8"
Yao Ming Shanghai, China Basketball	7'6"

Getting Serious

8   On her way to becoming a world champion, Biles faced tough decisions. In eighth grade, she was training 20 hours a week, far less than other elite gymnasts. If she wanted to be an Olympian, she would have to commit more time to training. For Biles, that meant shifting to homeschooling and taking on more practices. Traveling to competitions would be all business. A *Texas Monthly* story about Biles noted that when they travel "gymnasts are sequestered—they stay in a different hotel from the one in which their families stay—to reduce distractions. If they're allowed out at all, it's for carefully supervised visits to a tourist site or megamall." Still, Biles decided to make the switch. Afterwards, as she told Buzzfeed, "My hours ramped up and we did beam and bars twice a day, which usually I had only done once a day."

9   A few years later, she faced a similar choice when UCLA offered her a full athletic scholarship. To accept the scholarship and attend college with her peers, Biles would have to give up the opportunity for endorsement deals. The NCAA[3] doesn't allow student-athletes to make money off their names while they're in college. Biles once again decided to stick to professional gymnastics. As a professional, she could earn money and continue to face the world's top competition. Explaining her decision to Buzzfeed, Biles said, "I can always still go to college, but the window of opportunity of going professional is very [small] so I had to make a decision."

The Challenges of Fame

10   The first black gymnasts to win any medals during an Olympics competition were Dominique Dawes and Betty Okino in 1992. No black athlete won an individual gold medal at an Olympic gymnastics event until Gabby Douglas in 2012. Douglas, Dawes, and Okino were all subjected to racially-charged criticisms. Since she became a national figure, Biles has had to deal with similar issues. After she won the world championships in 2013, an Italian participant named Carlotta Ferlitto responded with negative comments. She said, "next time we should paint our skin black, so we could win, too." Instead of denouncing Ferlitto's remarks, an Italian spokesperson added, "the current trend in gymnastics . . . is going toward a technique that opens up new chances to athletes of color, well known for power, while penalizing the elegance typical of Eastern Europeans."

11   In October 2016, Biles appeared in a music video for the song "Overnight" with recording artist Jake Miller. In the video, Biles is portrayed as Miller's girlfriend. This led to negative comments about interracial relationships (Miller is white). It also led to outright racism directed at Biles. In response, she tweeted, "everyone forgets that I have feelings."

12   During the 2016 Olympics, Biles also faced intense media scrutiny about her family. She doesn't have a relationship with her biological father, and only occasionally speaks to her biological mother. She was briefly in foster care as a toddler. At age 5, she was adopted by her grandparents, Ron and Nellie Biles, whom she refers to as her parents. She didn't give her upbringing much thought until it became a topic of conversation at the Olympics. Biles told Buzzfeed that the interest in her family is "just kind of thrown at me and it's weird to talk about." Ultimately, she said in an interview with *Us Weekly,* "My parents are my parents, and that's it."

13   Racism and gossip have taken an emotional toll on Biles. Gymnastics can be mentally challenging. Training with tough coaches like Martha Karolyi, who oversees the U.S. women's team, makes it even tougher. According to *Texas*

Skill: Central or Main Idea

The heading makes me think another central idea is that Simone faced challenges throughout her career. The author explains the racial issues she had to deal with in 2013.

The details about Simone becoming a "national figure" and winning a world championship support and develop my first central idea.

---

3. **NCAA** the National Collegiate Athletic Association

Monthly, Biles started working with a sports psychologist named Robert Andrews to help in that area. She was afraid that something was "wrong" with her if she needed to talk to Andrews. He did his best to convince her that wasn't true, and that other top athletes also spoke to him about their anxieties. At first, not much changed. Biles hit a mental wall at the 2013 Secret U.S. Classic. It was her worst performance as a pro. As Buzzfeed describes it, "She fell from the uneven bars, bobbled on the beam, and almost fell off. Next came floor, typically her best piece, where she fell to her knees after a full-twisting double back somersault." Biles's longtime personal coach, Aimee Boorman, removed her from the rest of the competition for her own safety. "She could have done something that could've ended her career right then and there if I let her compete. I could tell that her mind wasn't where it needed to be," Boorman told Buzzfeed.

14   After that competition, Biles **invested** more time with Andrews. She also had some productive heart-to-hearts with Boorman and Karolyi. Her anxieties lessened. Now, she can often be seen laughing during events, while teammates and opponents are understandably more nervous. "I think I was just trying to live up to everyone's expectations that I kind of got lost in competing. I was just so stressed. I didn't know how to deal with a lot of it," Biles told Buzzfeed in the lead-up to the 2016 Olympics.

Not Done Yet

15   Biles is an exceptional athlete. Yet, her commitment to honing that athleticism in the gym and her willingness to make tough choices are what truly set her apart. Along the way, she has gracefully leapt over many hurdles. She has confronted racism and bullying. She has learned to accept the mental challenges that come with competing on the world's biggest stages. Few athletes have been able to stay so **resolute.**

16   Simone Biles isn't done either. She plans to continue participating in domestic and international gymnastics events. She has even hinted at a desire to make another Olympics run at the 2020 games in Tokyo, when she'll be 23. Regardless of whether she competes at the next Olympics, Simone Biles already exemplifies what it means to be an Olympic champion. In a sport where perfect-10 scores no longer exist, she's as close as they come to the perfect gymnast.

ALEX SHULTZ is a freelance writer from Plano, Texas. His work has appeared in Grantland, *Los Angeles Magazine*, the *Los Angeles Times* and *SLAM* magazine.

Please note that excerpts and passages in the StudySync® library and this workbook are intended as touchstones to generate interest in an author's work. The excerpts and passages do not substitute for the reading of entire texts, and StudySync® strongly recommends that students seek out and purchase the whole literary or informational work in order to experience it as the author intended. Links to online resellers are available in our digital library. In addition, complete works may be ordered through an authorized reseller by filling out and returning to StudySync® the order form enclosed in this workbook.

Reading & Writing Companion   55

First Read

Read "No Dream Too High: Simone Biles." After you read, complete the Think Questions below.

☁ THINK QUESTIONS

1. What does the anecdote in the first paragraph mainly tell readers about Simone Biles? Use specific evidence from the text to support your answer.

2. To what particular qualities or skills does the author of the text attribute Simone Biles's success? Similarly, which qualities might prove to be her own worst enemy? Cite examples of both in your response.

3. How has Simone Biles coped with the pressures of fame? Citing evidence from the text, explain how she has dealt with adversity in her life.

4. Based on context clues, what does the word **rigor** mean as it is used in the text? Write your best definition of *rigor* here, along with an explanation of how you inferred its meaning.

5. Read the following dictionary entry:

   invest
   in•vest \in'vest\ *verb*

   1. to spend money with the goal of making a profit
   2. to devote to something
   3. to provide with a particular quality or attribute

   Which definition most closely matches the meaning of **invested** as it is used in paragraph 14? Write the correct definition of *invested* here and explain how you figured it out.

Skill:
Central or Main Idea

Use the Checklist to analyze Central or Main Idea in "No Dream Too High: Simone Biles." Refer to the sample student annotations about Central or Main Idea in the text.

••• CHECKLIST FOR CENTRAL OR MAIN IDEA

In order to identify two or more central ideas in a text, note the following:

- ✓ the central or main idea, or ideas, if explicitly stated

- ✓ when each central idea appears

- ✓ key details in the text that indicate the author's point(s) or message(s)

- ✓ ways that the author uses details to develop a central idea

To determine two or more central ideas in a text and analyze their development over the course of the text, consider the following questions:

- ✓ What main ideas do the paragraphs develop?

- ✓ Where do you see more than one central idea for the text?

- ✓ How does the author use details to develop central ideas?

- ✓ How does the author develop these ideas over the course of the text?

- ✓ How might I objectively summarize the text, including the central ideas?

Skill:
Central or Main Idea

Reread paragraphs 15–16 of "No Dream Too High: Simone Biles." Then, using the Checklist on the previous page, answer the multiple-choice questions below.

↻ YOUR TURN

1. This question has two parts. First, answer Part A. Then, answer Part B.

   Part A: What statement best summarizes the two central ideas developed throughout the text?

   ○ A. Simone Biles was a struggling gymnast, and her willingness to work hard made her great.

   ○ B. Simone Biles is a fantastic gymnast, and she would be better if she worked harder.

   ○ C. Simone Biles is a talented and powerful gymnast whose natural gifts set her apart from other athletes in her sport.

   ○ D. Simone Biles is an amazing gymnast, and her ability to work hard and overcome obstacles is what makes her an incredible athlete.

   Part B: Select a sentence that best supports your answer to Part A.

   ○ A. Biles is an exceptional athlete.

   ○ B. Yet, her commitment to honing that athleticism in the gym and her willingness to make tough choices are what truly set her apart.

   ○ C. She has learned to accept the mental challenges that come with competing on the world's biggest stages.

   ○ D. In a sport where perfect-10 scores no longer exist, she's as close as they come to the perfect gymnast.

Close Read

Reread "No Dream Too High: Simone Biles." As you reread, complete the Skills Focus questions below. Then use your answers and annotations from the questions to help you complete the Write activity.

◎ SKILLS FOCUS

1. Find examples of facts, statistics, charts, or graphic aids in paragraphs 1 and 2. What do these examples suggest about the purpose of the paragraphs? What do they suggest about the author's opinion or view of Simone Biles?

2. Identify examples of the many challenges Simone has faced during her young career. What personal sacrifices did she make to achieve success?

3. This article develops two central or main ideas. Highlight evidence of these two central ideas, and explain them in your own words.

4. Identify evidence of how love drove Simone Biles to success and what she had to lose in order to succeed.

✎ WRITE

DEBATE: In this informational text, the author explains that Simone Biles made many sacrifices for the sport she loves. She often had to put gymnastics ahead of everything else. Would you choose a sport and fame over a normal life? What do you think is the better alternative? Prepare points and comments for a debate with your classmates. Use evidence from the text to support your point.

Please note that excerpts and passages in the StudySync® library and this workbook are intended as touchstones to generate interest in an author's work. The excerpts and passages do not substitute for the reading of entire texts, and StudySync® strongly recommends that students seek out and purchase the whole literary or informational work in order to experience it as the author intended. Links to online resellers are available in our digital library. In addition, complete works may be ordered through an authorized reseller by filling out and returning to StudySync® the order form enclosed in this workbook.

Reading & Writing Companion   **59**

The Highwayman

POETRY
Alfred Noyes
1906

Introduction

In the 18th century, highwaymen menaced England's rural roads. These robbers on horseback held up travelers, demanding that their victims "stand and deliver" their valuables. Yet England's highwaymen inspired sympathetic fascination along with fear. In this poem, Alfred Noyes (1880–1958) draws on the romantic lore of the highwayman to create a tragic scenario of love and sacrifice. Noyes also drew on his own memories of desolate Bagshot Heath in England, where

"And the highwayman came riding— Riding—riding—"

PART ONE

1 The wind was a **torrent** of darkness among the gusty trees.

2 The moon was a ghostly galleon[1] tossed upon cloudy seas.

3 The road was a ribbon of moonlight over the purple moor[2],

4 And the highwayman came riding—

5   Riding—riding—

6 The highwayman came riding, up to the old inn-door.

In "The Highwayman" by Alfred Noyes, a dashing robber on horseback wins the heart of Bess, whose father is the landlord of an inn.

7 He'd a French cocked-hat[3] on his forehead, a bunch of lace at his chin,

8 A coat of the claret[4] velvet, and breeches of brown doe-skin.

9 They fitted with never a wrinkle. His boots were up to the thigh.

10 And he rode with a jewelled twinkle,

11   His pistol butts a-twinkle,

12 His rapier hilt a-twinkle, under the jewelled sky.

13 Over the cobbles he **clattered** and clashed in the dark inn-yard.

14 He tapped with his whip on the shutters, but all was locked and barred.

15 He whistled a tune to the window, and who should be waiting there

16 But the landlord's black-eyed daughter,

17   Bess, the landlord's daughter,

18 Plaiting a dark red love-knot into her long black hair.

---

1. **galleon** an old, wooden war ship powered by sails
2. **moor** an expanse of boggy, grassy land
3. **French cocked-hat** a hat with a wide, stiff brim that is turned up in places toward the crown of the head
4. **claret** a dark maroon color

Skill:
Media

In both the poem and the video, the yard is dark. In the video, though, the light is shining around Bess. It makes her glow like a star or a diamond. This shows that Bess is the object of desire. Tim and the robber must be madly in love with her!

Skill:
Poetic Elements and Structure

There is alliteration of the letter "L." "L" has a soft and gentle sound that adds to the romantic feeling of the stanza.

19 And dark in the dark old inn-yard a stable-wicket creaked
20 Where Tim the ostler[5] listened. His face was white and peaked[6].
21 His eyes were hollows of madness, his hair like mouldy hay,
22 But he loved the landlord's daughter,
23   The landlord's red-lipped daughter.
24 Dumb as a dog he listened, and he heard the robber say—

25 "One kiss, my bonny sweetheart, I'm after a prize to-night,
26 But I shall be back with the yellow gold before the morning light;
27 Yet, if they press me sharply, and harry me through the day,
28 Then look for me by moonlight,
29   Watch for me by moonlight,
30 I'll come to thee by moonlight, though hell should bar the way."

31 He rose upright in the stirrups. He scarce could reach her hand,
32 But she loosened her hair in the casement. His face burnt like a brand
33 As the black cascade of perfume came tumbling over his breast;
34 And he kissed its waves in the moonlight,
35   (O, sweet black waves in the moonlight!)
36 Then he tugged at his rein in the moonlight, and galloped away to the west.

---

5. **ostler** a caretaker in charge of horses
6. **peaked** pale and sickly

PART TWO

37 He did not come in the dawning. He did not come at noon;
38 And out of the **tawny** sunset, before the rise of the moon,
39 When the road was a gypsy's ribbon, looping the purple moor,
40 A red-coat troop came marching—
41   Marching—marching—
42 King George's men came marching, up to the old inn-door.

43 They said no word to the landlord. They drank his ale instead.
44 But they gagged his daughter, and bound her, to the foot of her narrow bed.
45 Two of them knelt at her casement, with muskets at their side!
46 There was death at every window;
47   And hell at one dark window;
48 For Bess could see, through her casement, the road that *he* would ride.

49 They had tied her up to attention, with many a sniggering jest.
50 They had bound a musket beside her, with the muzzle beneath her breast!
51 "Now, keep good watch!" and they kissed her. She heard the doomed man say—
52 *Look for me by moonlight;*
53   *Watch for me by moonlight;*
54 *I'll come to thee by moonlight, though hell should bar the way!*

55 She twisted her hands behind her; but all the knots held good!
56 She writhed her hands till her fingers were wet with sweat or blood!
57 They stretched and strained in the darkness, and the hours crawled by like years
58 Till, now, on the stroke of midnight,
59   Cold, on the stroke of midnight,
60 The tip of one finger touched it! The trigger at least was hers!

61 The tip of one finger touched it. She strove no more for the rest.
62 Up, she stood up to attention, with the muzzle beneath her breast.
63 She would not risk their hearing; she would not **strive** again;
64 For the road lay bare in the moonlight;
65   Blank and bare in the moonlight;
66 And the blood of her veins, in the moonlight, throbbed to her love's refrain.

67 *Tlot-tlot; tlot-tlot!* Had they heard it? The horsehoofs ringing clear;
68 *Tlot-tlot; tlot-tlot,* in the distance? Were they deaf that they did not hear?
69 Down the ribbon of moonlight, over the brow of the hill,
70 The highwayman came riding—
71   Riding—riding—
72 The red coats looked to their priming! She stood up, straight and still.

Skill:
Media

This first part of the scene isn't in the poem at all, but it's kind of implied. The film shows Tim actually telling the redcoats about the highwayman. That's why they know to go to the old inn. It's much clearer what happened! Tim must have been jealous!

Skill:
Poetic Elements and Structure

The letter "T" is repeated at the end of a lot of words in this passage, which is consonance. The "T" sound sounds kind of like horse hooves and makes the poem feel more urgent as the robber gets closer.

73   *Tlot-tlot*, in the frosty silence! *Tlot-tlot*, in the echoing night!
74   Nearer he came and nearer. Her face was like a light.
75   Her eyes grew wide for a moment; she drew one last deep breath,
76   Then her finger moved in the moonlight,
77   Her musket shattered the moonlight,
78   Shattered her breast in the moonlight and warned him—with her death.

79   He turned. He spurred to the west; he did not know who stood
80   Bowed, with her head o'er the musket, drenched with her own blood!
81   Not till the dawn he heard it, and his face grew grey to hear
82   How Bess, the landlord's daughter,
83   The landlord's black-eyed daughter,
84   Had watched for her love in the moonlight, and died in the darkness there.

85   Back, he spurred like a madman, shrieking a curse to the sky,
86   With the white road smoking behind him and his rapier **brandished** high.
87   Blood red were his spurs in the golden noon; wine-red was his velvet coat;
88   When they shot him down on the highway,
89   Down like a dog on the highway,
90   And he lay in his blood on the highway, with a bunch of lace at his throat.

. . .

91   *And still of a winter's night, they say, when the wind is in the trees,*
92   *When the moon is a ghostly galleon tossed upon cloudy seas,*
93   *When the road is a ribbon of moonlight over the purple moor,*
94   *A highwayman comes riding—*
95   *Riding—riding—*
96   *A highwayman comes riding, up to the old inn-door.*

97   *Over the cobbles he clatters and clangs in the dark inn-yard.*
98   *He taps with his whip on the shutters, but all is locked and barred.*
99   *He whistles a tune to the window, and who should be waiting there*
100   *But the landlord's black-eyed daughter,*
101   *Bess, the landlord's daughter,*
102   *Plaiting a dark red love-knot into her long black hair.*

First Read

Read "The Highwayman." After you read, complete the Think Questions below.

THINK QUESTIONS

1. A love triangle is a situation in which two people love the same third person. What love triangle exists in "The Highwayman"? Cite textual evidence from the selection to support your answer.

2. How do King George's men treat Bess, and why do they treat her that way? Cite textual evidence from the selection to support your answer.

3. How does the highwayman respond when he hears about Bess's death? Cite textual evidence from the selection to support your answer.

4. Find the word **strive** in line 63 of "The Highwayman." Use context clues in the surrounding sentences, as well as the sentence in which the word appears, to determine the word's meaning. Write your definition here and identify clues that helped you figure out the meaning.

5. Use context clues to determine the meaning of **brandish** as it is used in line 86 of "The Highwayman." Write your definition here and identify clues that helped you figure out the meaning. Then check the meaning in a dictionary.

Please note that excerpts and passages in the StudySync® library and this workbook are intended as touchstones to generate interest in an author's work. The excerpts and passages do not substitute for the reading of entire texts, and StudySync® strongly recommends that students seek out and purchase the whole literary or informational work in order to experience it as the author intended. Links to online resellers are available in our digital library. In addition, complete works may be ordered through an authorized reseller by filling out and returning to StudySync® the order form enclosed in this workbook.

Reading & Writing Companion   **65**

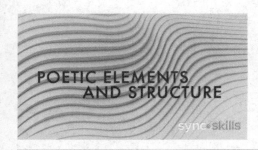

Skill:
Poetic Elements and Structure

Use the Checklist to analyze Poetic Elements and Structure in "The Highwayman." Refer to the sample student annotations about Poetic Elements and Structure in the text.

••• CHECKLIST FOR POETIC ELEMENTS AND STRUCTURE

In order to identify poetic elements and structure, note the following:

✓ the form and overall structure of the poem

✓ the rhyme, rhythm, and meter, if present

✓ lines and stanzas in the poem that suggest its meaning

✓ other sound elements, such as:

• alliteration: the repetition of initial consonant sounds, as with the *s* sound in "Cindy sweeps the sand"

• consonance: the repetition of consonant sounds in the middle and ends of words, as with the *t* sound in "little bats in the attic"

• assonance: the repetition of vowel sounds in words, as with the long *e* sound in "dreams of bees and sheep"

To analyze the impact of rhymes and other repetitions of sounds on a specific verse or stanza of a poem, consider the following questions:

✓ What sound elements are present in specific stanzas of the poem?

✓ What is the effect of different sound elements on the stanza or verse?

Skill:
Poetic Elements and Structure

Reread lines 1–30 from Part One of "The Highwayman." Then, complete the chart on the next page by identifying the effect each sound element has on the verse or stanza.

⟳ YOUR TURN

	Letter Bank
A	Repeating the same harsh *C* sound makes the sound of a horse on a road, creating an urgent or excited mood.
B	The repetitions of *K* sounds remind me of how the creak disturbs the silence.
C	The repetition of the *R* sound makes this verse sound like it's flowing, like the ribbon of road and the highwayman's riding.
D	The repeated *G* sound emphasizes the moon and has a gutteral sound that mirrors the stormy imagery.
E	The repeated sound -*inkle* in the description of the highwayman's appearance makes him seem less dangerous because -*inkle* is a funny and whimsical sound.

Please note that excerpts and passages in the StudySync® library and this workbook are intended as touchstones to generate interest in an author's work. The excerpts and passages do not substitute for the reading of entire texts, and StudySync® strongly recommends that students seek out and purchase the whole literary or informational work in order to experience it as the author intended. Links to online resellers are available in our digital library. In addition, complete works may be ordered through an authorized reseller by filling out and returning to StudySync® the order form enclosed in this workbook.

Reading & Writing
Companion

67

Text	Sound Element	Effect on Verse or Stanza
The moon was a ghostly galleon tossed upon cloudy seas.	alliteration	
The road was a ribbon of moonlight over the purple moor, And the highwayman came riding— Riding—riding— The highwayman came riding, up to the old inn-door.	consonance	
They fitted with never a wrinkle. His boots were up to the thigh. And he rode with a jewelled twinkle, His pistol butts a-twinkle, His rapier hilt a-twinkle, under the jewelled sky.	rhyme	
Over the cobbles he clattered and clashed in the dark inn-yard.	alliteration	
And dark in the dark old inn-yard a stable-wicket creaked Where Tim the ostler listened. His face was white and peaked.	consonance	

Skill:
Media

Use the Checklist to analyze Media in "The Highwayman." Refer to the sample student annotations about Media in the text.

••• CHECKLIST FOR MEDIA

In order to determine how to compare and contrast a written story, drama, or poem to its audio, filmed, staged, or multimedia version, do the following:

✓ choose a story that has been presented in multiple forms of media, such as a written story and a film adaptation

✓ note techniques that are unique to each medium—print, audio, and video:

- lighting

- sound

- color

- tone and style

- camera focus and angles

- word choice

- structure

✓ examine how these techniques may have an effect on the story and its ideas, as well as the reader's, listener's, or viewer's understanding of the work as a whole

✓ examine similarities and differences between the written story and its audio or video version

To compare and contrast a written story, drama, or poem to its audio, filmed, staged, or multimedia version, analyzing the effects of techniques unique to each medium, consider the following questions:

✓ How do different types of media treat story elements?

✓ What techniques are unique to each medium—print, audio, and video?

✓ How does the medium—for example, a film's use of music, sound, and camera angles—affect a person's understanding of the work as a whole?

Skill:
Media

Reread lines 1–14 of "The Highwayman," and then view this same scene from the video clip of "The Highwayman." Then, using the Checklist on the previous page, answer the multiple-choice questions below and on the next page.

♺ YOUR TURN

1. This question has two parts. First, answer Part A. Then, answer Part B.

   Part A: Which of the following details in the film version of "The Highwayman" is different from the printed text?

   ○ A. The inn-yard is well lit in the film version.

   ○ B. The highwayman is walking instead of riding in the film.

   ○ C. The stanza describing the highwayman's appearance is missing in the film.

   ○ D. The film version seems light and happy, and the poem seems dark and moody.

   Part B: Which of the following BEST explains why the film version might have presented this detail in Part A in a different way?

   ○ A. The missing stanza described things that wouldn't make sense to modern audiences.

   ○ B. The description of the highwayman's appearance is unnecessary in the film because the viewer can see him.

   ○ C. The clothes described in the poem would have been expensive, and the film couldn't afford to show them.

   ○ D. The filmmakers didn't want to show the weapons described in the missing stanza.

2. Which film element best helps you to understand that the story takes place hundreds of years ago?

   ○ A. The film uses different types of lighting.

   ○ B. The film begins by focusing on objects such as a candle, a tin cup, and a leather boot.

   ○ C. The narrator says that this event takes places hundreds of years ago.

   ○ D. The film does not use film elements to help you understand the time or setting.

3. How does the film use lighting to affect your understanding of the highwayman in the opening scene?

   ○ A. The highwayman is filmed in darker lighting, suggesting he may be unwelcome or dangerous.

   ○ B. The highwayman is filmed in bright lighting, suggesting he may be a hero.

   ○ C. The highwayman is filmed in various lightning, suggesting that he may be a complex character.

   ○ D. The film does not use lighting to help you better understand the highwayman.

Please note that excerpts and passages in the StudySync® library and this workbook are intended as touchstones to generate interest in an author's work. The excerpts and passages do not substitute for the reading of entire texts, and StudySync® strongly recommends that students seek out and purchase the whole literary or informational work in order to experience it as the author intended. Links to online resellers are available in our digital library. In addition, complete works may be ordered through an authorized reseller by filling out and returning to StudySync® the order form enclosed in this workbook.

Reading & Writing
Companion

71

Close Read

Reread "The Highwayman." As you reread, complete the Skills Focus questions below. Then use your answers and annotations from the questions to help you complete the Write activity.

◎ SKILLS FOCUS

1. Identify two or three examples of different sound patterns (alliteration, consonance, assonance) in the poem. Explain how these sounds affect the poem's feeling and meaning.

2. Identify two or three examples of rhymes. Explain how they affect the poem's mood.

3. One of the film elements used in the video is lighting. Identify and explain moments where the meaning or tone of the poem is made more clear by the lighting in the film.

4. Identify Bess's final action. Explain what readers can learn about love and loss from the relationship in the poem.

✎ WRITE

LITERARY ANALYSIS: "The Highwayman" is a poem full of different emotions and moods. Identify lines or stanzas in the poem where the mood shifts. How does the poem use sound repetition and other poetic elements to show these changes? How does the film show and enhance these changes in mood? Write a response to answer these questions, analyzing the techniques unique to each medium. Remember to use evidence from the poem and the filmed adaptation.

Flesh and Blood So Cheap:

The Triangle Fire and Its Legacy

INFORMATIONAL TEXT
Albert Marrin
2011

Introduction

The Triangle Shirtwaist Factory fire in 1911 was the most lethal workplace tragedy in American history until the attack on the World Trade Center on September 11, 2001. The Lower Manhattan blaze killed 146 workers, most of them young, female immigrants of Jewish and Italian descent. Author Albert Marrin traces the history of the garment industry, exploring the immigrant experience of the early 1900s, including the sweatshop conditions many new arrivals to America were forced to endure. The Triangle Fire prompted activists to lobby for reforms, resulting in improved safety standards and working conditions that we now take

"Onlookers saw many dreadful sights, none more so than the end of a love affair."

Skill:
Informational
Text Structure

The author is explaining how the fire grew with cause-and-effect structure. Burning fabric caused other pieces to catch on fire. Since the hose was not connected, no water came out, and the fire grew. This is an example of how poor safety standards resulted in tragedy.

Excerpt from Chapter V

Holocaust

1   We will never know for sure what started the Triangle Fire. Most likely, a cutter[1] flicked a hot ash or tossed a live cigarette butt into a scrap bin. Whatever the cause, survivors said the first sign of trouble was smoke pouring from beneath a cutting table.

2   Cutters flung buckets of water at the smoking spot, without effect. Flames shot up, **igniting** the line of hanging paper patterns. "They began to fall on the layers of thin goods underneath them," recalled cutter Max Rothen. "Every time another piece dropped, light scraps of burning fabric began to fly around the room. They came down on the other tables and they fell on the machines. Then the line broke and the whole string of burning patterns fell down." A foreman ran for the hose on the stairway wall. Nothing! No water came. The hose had not been connected to the **standpipe.** Seconds later, the fire leaped out of control.

3   Yet help was already on the way. At exactly 4:45 p.m., someone pulled the eighth-floor fire alarm. In less than two minutes, the horse-drawn vehicles of Engine Company 72 arrived from a firehouse six blocks away. The moment they arrived, the firefighters unloaded their equipment and prepared to swing into action. As they did, the area pumping station raised water pressure in the hydrants near the Asch Building. Other units soon arrived from across the Lower East Side with more equipment.

The Triangle Shirtwaist Factory fire is the deadliest industrial disaster in U.S. history. The factory was located on the eighth, ninth, and tenth floors of the Asch building in New York City.

---

1. **cutter** a person who works at a table in a clothing factory

4   Meanwhile, workers on the eighth floor rang furiously for the two passenger elevators. Safety experts have always advised against using elevators in a fire. Heat can easily damage their machinery, leaving trapped passengers dangling in space, to burn or **suffocate.** Despite the danger, the operators made several trips, saving scores of workers before heat bent the elevators' tracks and put them out of action.

5   Those who could not board elevators rushed the stairway door. They caused a pileup so that those in front could not open the door. Whenever someone tried to get it open, the crowd pinned her against it. "All the girls were falling on me and they squeezed me to the door," Ida Willensky recalled. "Three times I said to the girls, 'Please, girls, let me open the door. Please!' But they would not listen to me." Finally, cutter Louis Brown barged through the crowd and forced the door open.

6   Workers, shouting, crying, and gasping for air, slowly made their way downstairs. There were no lights in the stairway, so they had to grope their way in darkness. A girl fell; others fell on top of her, blocking the stairs until firefighters arrived moments later. Yet everyone who took the stairway from the eighth floor got out alive, exiting through the Washington Place doors. Those on the ninth floor were not so lucky.

• • •

7   Those who reached the ninth-floor stairway door found it locked. This was not unusual, as employers often locked doors to discourage latecomers and keep out union organizers[2]. "My God, I am lost!" cried Margaret Schwartz as her hair caught fire. Nobody who went to that door survived, nor any who reached the windows.

8   With a wave of fire rolling across the room, workers rushed to the windows, only to meet more fire. Hot air expands. Unless it escapes, pressure will keep building, eventually blowing a hole even in a heavy iron container like a boiler. Heat and pressure blew out the eighth-floor windows. Firefighters call the result "lapping in"—that is sucking flames into open windows above. That is why you see black scorch marks on the wall above the window of a burnt out room.

9   With fire advancing from behind and flames rising before them, people knew they were doomed. Whatever they did meant certain death. By remaining in the room, they chose death by fire or suffocation. Jumping ninety-five feet to the ground meant death on the sidewalk. We cannot know what passed through the minds of those who decided to jump. Yet their thinking, in those

2. **union organizers** people who recruit workers to organize under a union's banner

last moments of life, may have gone like this: If I jump, my family will have a body to identify and bury, but if I stay in this room, there will be nothing left.

10 A girl clung to a window frame until flames from the eighth floor lapped in, burning her face and setting fire to her hair and clothing. She let go. Just then, Frances Perkins reached the scene from her friend's town house on the north side of Washington Square. "Here they come," onlookers shouted as Engine Company 72 reined in their horses. "Don't jump; stay there." Seconds later, Hook and Ladder Company 20 arrived.

11 Firefighters charged into the building, stretching a hose up the stairways as they went. At the sixth-floor landing, they connected it to the standpipe. Reaching the eighth floor, they crawled into the **inferno** on their bellies, under the rising smoke, with their hose. Yet nothing they did could save those at the windows. Photos of the portable towers show streams of water playing on the top three floors. (A modern high-pressure pumper can send water as high as one thousand feet.) Plenty of water got through the windows, but not those with people standing in them. A burst of water under high pressure would have hurled them backward, into the flames.

12 Hoping to catch jumpers before they hit the ground, firefighters held up life nets, sturdy ten-foot-square nets made of rope. It was useless. A person falling from the ninth floor struck with a force equal to eleven thousand pounds. Some jumpers bounced off the nets, dying when they hit the ground; others tore the nets, crashing through to the pavement. "The force was so great it took men off their feet," said Captain Howard Ruch of Engine Company 18. "Trying to hold the nets, the men turned somersaults. The men's hands were bleeding, the nets were torn and some caught fire" from burning clothing. Officers, fearing their men would be struck by falling bodies, ordered the nets removed. The **aerial** ladders failed, too, reaching only to the sixth floor. **Desperate** jumpers tried to grab hold of a rung on the way down, missed, and landed on the sidewalk.

. . .

13 Onlookers saw many dreadful sights, none more so than the end of a love affair. A young man appeared at a window. Gently, he helped a young woman step onto the windowsill, held her away from the building—and let go. He helped another young woman onto the windowsill. "Those of us who were looking saw her put her arms around him and kiss him," Shepherd wrote. "Then he held her out into space and dropped her. But quick as a flash he was on the windowsill himself. . . . He was brave enough to help the girl he loved to a quicker death, after she had given him a goodbye kiss."

. . .

14 By 5:15 p.m., exactly thirty-five minutes after flames burst from beneath a cutting table, firefighters had brought the blaze under control. An hour later, Chief Croker made his inspection. He found that the Asch Building had no damage to its structure. Its walls were in good shape; so were the floors. It had passed the test. It was fireproof.

15 The woodwork, furniture, cotton goods, and people who worked in it were not. Of the 500 Triangle employees who reported for work that day, 146 died. Of these, sixteen men were identified. The rest were women or bodies and body parts listed as "unidentified." The Triangle Fire was New York's worst workplace disaster up to that time. Only the September 11, 2001, terrorist attacks on the twin towers of the World Trade Center took more (about 2,500) lives.

Excerpted from *Flesh and Blood So Cheap: The Triangle Fire and Its Legacy* by Albert Marrin, published by Alfred A. Knopf.

Skill:
Informational
Text Structure

He talks about exact times. This is a sequential text structure. This shows how important time was in this tragedy. So much life was lost in a short time. This is why safety at work is so important.

First Read

Read *Flesh and Blood So Cheap: The Triangle Fire and Its Legacy*. After you read, complete the Think Questions below.

☁ THINK QUESTIONS

1. What happened at the Triangle Shirtwaist Factory? What caused it? Cite evidence to support your response.

2. Which floor had the most casualties? Why? Be sure to cite evidence from the text in your response.

3. **Mood** is the emotional quality or atmosphere of a story or poem. What is the mood of this text? Support your answer with examples of language from the text.

4. Use context clues to determine the meaning of **standpipe** as it is used in paragraph 2 of *Flesh and Blood So Cheap: The Triangle Fire and Its Legacy*. Write your definition here and identify clues that helped you figure out the meaning.

5. Read the following dictionary entry:

   inferno
   in•fer•no *noun*

   1. a large fire that burns out of control
   2. Hell, or a place like it

   How does the use of **inferno** in *Flesh and Blood So Cheap: The Triangle Fire and Its Legacy* match both definitions? Explain how you figured out both meanings.

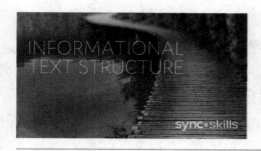

Skill:
Informational Text Structure

Use the Checklist to analyze Informational Text Structure in *Flesh and Blood So Cheap: The Triangle Fire and Its Legacy*. Refer to the sample student annotations about Informational Text Structure in the text.

••• CHECKLIST FOR INFORMATIONAL TEXT STRUCTURE

In order to determine the overall structure of a text, note the following:

✓ the topic(s) and how the author organizes information about the topic(s)

✓ patterns in a section of text that reveal the text structure, such as:

- sequences, including the order of events or steps in a process
- problems and their solutions
- cause-and-effect relationships
- comparisons

✓ the overall structure of the text and how each section contributes to the development of ideas

To analyze the structure an author uses to organize a text, including how the major sections contribute to the whole and to the development of the ideas, use the following questions as a guide:

✓ What organizational pattern does the author use? How does it reveal the text structure used to present information?

✓ How does a particular section fit into the overall structure of the text? How does it contribute to the whole and the development of the author's ideas?

✓ In what ways does the text structure contribute to the development of ideas in the text?

Please note that excerpts and passages in the StudySync® library and this workbook are intended as touchstones to generate interest in an author's work. The excerpts and passages do not substitute for the reading of entire texts, and StudySync® strongly recommends that students seek out and purchase the whole literary or informational work in order to experience it as the author intended. Links to online resellers are available in our digital library. In addition, complete works may be ordered through an authorized reseller by filling out and returning to StudySync® the order form enclosed in this workbook.

Reading & Writing Companion

79

Skill:
Informational Text Structure

Reread paragraphs 6–7 of *Flesh and Blood So Cheap: The Triangle Fire and Its Legacy*. Then, using the Checklist on the previous page, answer the multiple-choice questions below.

⟳ YOUR TURN

---

1. This question has two parts. First, answer Part A. Then, answer Part B.

   Part A: Which of the following best describes the structure the author uses to organize the two paragraphs?

   ○ A. sequence

   ○ B. problem-and-solution

   ○ C. cause-and-effect

   ○ D. comparison-and-contrast

   Part B: Which sentence from the excerpt supports your answer to Part A?

   ○ A. "Those on the ninth floor were not so lucky."

   ○ B. "Those who reached the ninth-floor stairway door found it locked."

   ○ C. "There were no lights in the stairway, so they had to grope their way in darkness."

   ○ D. "Workers, shouting, crying, and gasping for air, slowly made their way downstairs."

2. How does the text structure contribute to the development of the author's ideas about workplace safety?

   ○ A. By giving an example of how there were not safety standards throughout the building

   ○ B. By giving a detailed description of how the fire spread on the factory floor

   ○ C. By explaining that the Triangle Shirtwaist Factory fire was a workplace disaster

   ○ D. By focusing on the exact times the events unfolded

Close Read

Reread *Flesh and Blood So Cheap: The Triangle Fire and Its Legacy.* As you reread, complete the Skills Focus questions below. Then use your answers and annotations from the questions to help you complete the Write activity.

◎ SKILLS FOCUS

1. Explain how and why the author uses a cause-and-effect text structure in paragraph 4. Highlight evidence from the text and make annotations to explain your reasoning.

2. In paragraphs 6 and 7, Marrin compares and contrasts what happened to the workers on the eighth and ninth floors. What other text structure does he use in sentences 2–4 of paragraph 6? Highlight the transition word in sentence 2, and make annotations to label the text structure.

3. What text structure does the author use in paragraph 9? How does this organizational structure contribute to the development of ideas? Highlight evidence and make annotations to explain your answer.

4. The tragedy of the Triangle Fire resulted in the loss of many lives. Find evidence from the text that shows reasons why so many workers died so quickly in the fire. In your own words, explain how these deaths could have been prevented.

✎ WRITE

INFORMATIVE: Author Albert Marrin explains how poor working conditions and greedy bosses led to the tragedy at the Triangle Shirtwaist Factory. Identify sections that contribute to the development of this idea. Then analyze the text structures Marrin uses to organize those sections. Support your response with specific examples from the text.

Please note that excerpts and passages in the StudySync® library and this workbook are intended as touchstones to generate interest in an author's work. The excerpts and passages do not substitute for the reading of entire texts, and StudySync® strongly recommends that students seek out and purchase the whole literary or informational work in order to experience it as the author intended. Links to online resellers are available in our digital library. In addition, complete works may be ordered through an authorized reseller by filling out and returning to StudySync® the order form enclosed in this workbook.

Reading & Writing Companion   81

A Christmas Carol

FICTION
Charles Dickens
1843

Introduction

Set in 19th-century London, Charles Dickens's short novel *A Christmas Carol* is considered by many to be one of the most influential works of fiction ever written. In this memorable story, the compassionate Dickens (1812–1870) paints a vivid portrayal of the cold-hearted miser Ebenezer Scrooge, the very embodiment of despair and darkness. Though he will be given a chance to change his ways, in this passage from early in the book, we find Scrooge in his "counting-house" obsessed with ledgers and coins and berating his cheerful nephew on the foolishness of Christmas.

"'Bah!' said Scrooge, 'Humbug!'"

NOTES

from Stave I: Marley's Ghost

1   Once upon a time—of all the good days in the year, on Christmas Eve—old Scrooge sat busy in his counting-house[1]. It was cold, bleak, biting weather: foggy withal: and he could hear the people in the court outside, go wheezing up and down, beating their hands upon their breasts, and stamping their feet upon the pavement stones to warm them. The city clocks had only just gone three, but it was quite dark already—it had not been light all day—and candles were flaring in the windows of the neighbouring offices, like ruddy smears upon the **palpable** brown air. The fog came pouring in at every chink and keyhole, and was so dense without, that although the court was of the narrowest, the houses opposite were mere phantoms. To see the dingy cloud come drooping down, obscuring everything, one might have thought that Nature lived hard by, and was brewing on a large scale.

2   The door of Scrooge's counting-house was open that he might keep his eye upon his clerk[2], who in a dismal little cell beyond, a sort of tank, was copying letters. Scrooge had a very small fire, but the clerk's fire was so very much smaller that it looked like one coal. But he couldn't replenish it, for Scrooge kept the coal-box[3] in his own room; and so surely as the clerk came in with the shovel, the master predicted that it would be necessary for them to part. Wherefore the clerk put on his white comforter, and tried to warm himself at the candle; in which effort, not being a man of a strong imagination, he failed.

3   "A merry Christmas, uncle! God save you!" cried a cheerful voice. It was the voice of Scrooge's nephew, who came upon him so quickly that this was the first **intimation** he had of his approach.

4   "Bah!" said Scrooge, "Humbug!"

---

1. **counting-house** a building or an office used for keeping books
2. **clerk** a worker who keeps records or books of accounts and finance
3. **coal-box** a box that holds coal before it is used in a fire or furnace

NOTES

5   He had so heated himself with rapid walking in the fog and frost, this nephew of Scrooge's, that he was all in a glow; his face was ruddy and handsome; his eyes sparkled, and his breath smoked again.

6   "Christmas a humbug, uncle!" said Scrooge's nephew. "You don't mean that, I am sure?"

7   "I do," said Scrooge. "Merry Christmas! What right have you to be merry? What reason have you to be merry? You're poor enough."

8   "Come, then," returned the nephew gaily. "What right have you to be dismal? What reason have you to be morose? You're rich enough."

9   Scrooge having no better answer ready on the spur of the moment, said, "Bah!" again; and followed it up with "Humbug."

10   "Don't be cross, uncle!" said the nephew.

11   "What else can I be," returned the uncle, "when I live in such a world of fools as this? Merry Christmas! Out upon merry Christmas! What's Christmas time to you but a time for paying bills without money; a time for finding yourself a year older, but not an hour richer; a time for balancing your books and having every item in 'em through a round dozen of months presented dead against you? If I could work my will," said Scrooge **indignantly,** "every idiot who goes about with 'Merry Christmas' on his lips, should be boiled with his own pudding, and buried with a stake of holly through his heart. He should!"

12   "Uncle!" pleaded the nephew.

13   "Nephew!" returned the uncle sternly, "keep Christmas in your own way, and let me keep it in mine."

14   "Keep it!" repeated Scrooge's nephew. "But you don't keep it."

15   "Let me leave it alone, then," said Scrooge. "Much good may it do you! Much good it has ever done you!"

16   "There are many things from which I might have **derived** good, by which I have not profited, I dare say," returned the nephew. "Christmas among the rest. But I am sure I have always thought of Christmas time, when it has come round—apart from the veneration due to its sacred name and origin, if anything belonging to it can be apart from that—as a good time; a kind, forgiving, charitable, pleasant time; the only time I know of, in the long calendar of the year, when men and women seem by one consent to open their shut-up hearts freely, and to think of people below them as if they really

were fellow-passengers to the grave, and not another race of creatures bound on other journeys. And therefore, uncle, though it has never put a scrap of gold or silver in my pocket, I believe that it has done me good, and will do me good; and I say, God bless it!"

17   The clerk in the Tank involuntarily applauded. Becoming immediately sensible of the **impropriety,** he poked the fire, and extinguished the last frail spark for ever.

18   "Let me hear another sound from *you*," said Scrooge, "and you'll keep your Christmas by losing your situation! You're quite a powerful speaker, sir," he added, turning to his nephew. "I wonder you don't go into Parliament."

19   "Don't be angry, uncle. Come! Dine with us to-morrow."

20   Scrooge said that he would see him—yes, indeed he did. He went the whole length of the expression, and said that he would see him in that extremity first.

21   "But why?" cried Scrooge's nephew. "Why?"

22   "Why did you get married?" said Scrooge.

23   "Because I fell in love."

24   "Because you fell in love!" growled Scrooge, as if that were the only one thing in the world more ridiculous than a merry Christmas. "Good afternoon!"

25   "Nay, uncle, but you never came to see me before that happened. Why give it as a reason for not coming now?"

26   "Good afternoon," said Scrooge.

27   "I want nothing from you; I ask nothing of you; why cannot we be friends?"

28   "Good afternoon," said Scrooge.

29   "I am sorry, with all my heart, to find you so **resolute.** We have never had any quarrel, to which I have been a party. But I have made the trial in homage[4] to Christmas, and I'll keep my Christmas humour to the last. So A Merry Christmas, uncle!"

30   "Good afternoon!" said Scrooge.

31   "And A Happy New Year!"

---

4. **homage** an expression of deep respect and admiration; honor

32 "Good afternoon!" said Scrooge.

33 His nephew left the room without an angry word, notwithstanding. He stopped at the outer door to bestow the greetings of the season on the clerk, who, cold as he was, was warmer than Scrooge; for he returned them cordially[5].

✎ WRITE

PERSONAL NARRATIVE: The excerpt from *A Christmas Carol* depicts a conflict between an uncle and his nephew during Christmas. Write about a time of conflict during a holiday in your own family. At the end of your narrative, provide a conclusion that follows from and reflects on the experience. Consider how the conflict affected you and your family. What did you learn about love and loss?

---

5. **cordially** politely; in a friendly way

Tangerine

FICTION
Edward Bloor
1997

Introduction

Even though he's legally blind, 12-year-old Paul Fisher can see quite a bit through his bug-eyed, Coke-bottle glasses. His parents don't always do as they say. His beloved sports-star brother, Erik, is a self-absorbed bully. And the town the Fishers have moved to—Lake Windsor Downs, in Tangerine County, Florida—might just be the strangest place on Earth. So strange, in fact, that Paul begins to wonder if it might just be the place for a four-eyed zero to transform himself into a certified hero. In this excerpt from the critically acclaimed young adult novel by Edward Bloor (b. 1950), Paul looks on as his brother's football dreams

"This is the house built on the Erik Fisher Football Dream."

1   The third quarter was as dull as the first two, but Cypress Bay's offense suddenly got it together in the final period. They drove eighty-five yards for a touchdown, most of those yards coming from that big fullback. The kick for the extra point was good, and Cypress Bay led 7–0.

2   Antoine responded with two short runs and then a beautiful forty-yard pass to Terry Donnelly, who was wide open down the left sideline. I could have caught that pass. My grandmother could have caught it, for that matter, but Terry Donnelly dropped it. Antoine had to punt again.

3   That's when I noticed the black clouds rolling in. That whole mess with the visitors' bleachers and Mr. Bridges and the cops had pushed the game past the four o'clock **barrier.** In a matter of minutes we went from sunny skies to *kaboom!* And then down it came, a hard, cold rain. Most of the fans climbed down from the bleachers and ran for their cars. Mom yelled, "Come on, you two!" but Dad said, "No, you go ahead. I'm staying," so I said, "I'm staying, too."

4   Mom was already on the ground. She yelled back, "Fine. Stay. I hope neither of you gets killed." She ran back to the Volvo, leaving us to get soaked. Or worse.

5   The rain turned out to be a blessing for Lake Windsor. The offensive line started pushing Cypress Bay back, letting Antoine move the ball steadily down the field—five yards, six yards, five yards, seven yards. With two minutes to play, the Seagulls were all the way down to the Cypress Bay five-yard line. Antoine faked a run to the right and **lofted** a pass into the left corner of the end zone that some mud-covered Seagull receiver caught for a touchdown. A soggy cheer went up from the few fans left in the bleachers. The score was 7–6, and Erik's big moment had arrived.

6   He came running onto the field in his perfectly clean, mud-free uniform to kick the extra point that would tie the game. Erik had never missed a point. Never. I was expecting to see Arthur Bauer trotting out with him, but number 4 was still standing there on the sideline with the other clean uniforms.

NOTES

7   The two muddy teams lined up. Erik got into his kicking stance, and Antoine Thomas crouched down in front of him to hold the ball. I said, "Check it out, Dad. Antoine's the holder."

8   "I see," he said grimly. "Erik told me that Arthur would be his holder. I don't think it's such a good idea to throw a surprise like this at your kicker."

9   Dad, and Erik, and I, and everybody else figured that Arthur had taken over Mike Costello's job. But no. There was Antoine, in the crouch, getting ready to spin the laces and set the ball down for Erik.

10   The referee blew his whistle, the clock started to tick, and Lake Windsor's big center snapped the ball. Erik, his head down in total concentration, took two steps forward, like he's rehearsed a million times. His foot started toward the ball in a powerful arc, and then—the most incredible thing happened. Antoine whipped the ball away at the last second, like Lucy does with Charlie Brown. He took off running around the right side and crossed the goal line, untouched, for a two-point conversion. Seagulls led 8–7.

11   At the same moment, Erik, who clearly did not expect Antoine to pull the ball away, kicked at nothing but the air. His left foot went flying off in one direction, his right foot in another. For a split second he was a **parallel** line three feet above the ground. Then he made a perfect banana-peel back-flop landing in the mud. The people around us started laughing, hooting, and cheering, all at the same time. Antoine spiked the ball in the end zone, and all the Lake Windsor players, except Erik, ran over and jumped on him. All the Lake Windsor players on the sideline, except Arthur, started jumping up and down, too.

12   Erik finally got up and walked to the sideline to get his kicking tee. His front was still clean and white, but his back was now filthy. He kicked the ball back to the Cardinals, but they fumbled it away, and that's how it ended. Lake Windsor 8, Cypress Bay 7.

13   When we got back to the car, Mom just said, "From here, it sounded like we won."

14   I wanted to tell her all about Erik's banana-peel back-flop special, but Dad cut in right away. "Yes. We won on a fake kick. They sent Erik out to fake the kick for the extra point. That drew the offense to him, and it cleared the way for Antoine to run it in for two points."

15   Mom thought for a minute. "So Erik did something that helped win the game."

NOTES

16   "Most definitely," Dad said. "It's not something that shows up in the stats in the newspapers. It's not something people will remember. But it helped win the game."

17   I thought to myself, *Not remember? You've got to be kidding. Erik's flying banana-peel back-flop in the mud is the one thing about this game that everybody is going to remember.*

18   Dad continued talking in this manner throughout dinner, pounding home his theme to Erik—that Erik had contributed big-time to the victory, that Erik had actually made victory possible by being the **decoy.** I don't think Erik was even listening. He was just sitting there, looking down, twisting his varsity ring[1] around and around his finger.

19   After dinner Dad flipped on the TV so we could all watch the local news. The lead story on channel 2 was the revolt of the Cypress Bay fans and their brief takeover of the **condemned** visitors' bleachers.

20   About two-thirds of the way through the broadcast came "The Saturday Sports Roundup." The sports anchorman went through the professional baseball and football stuff, then the college football scores, and then the high school scores. "Lake Windsor 8, Cypress Bay 7."

21   The broadcast ended with a feature called "The Weak in Sports." It was a collection of sports bloopers, and guess who they saved for last.

22   The anchorman said something like, "Finally, a play that looks like it was drawn up by the Three Stooges. Watch closely." And there it was. A ground-level view of the ball being snapped to Antoine, of Erik striding forward confidently, and *Whooo!* Up in the air he flew! It was even more comical than I had remembered. Erik went splashing down into the mud, but he didn't stay there. They rewound the tape so that he popped back up, flopped again, popped back up, and flopped again. Finally, the camera turned toward the end zone to catch Antoine spiking the ball. It zoomed in on his face. Antoine was laughing and pointing his finger at the big center, who was pointing back at him.

23   When the anchorman came back on, he was cracking up. So were all the other news people. The credits started rolling, and they started saying stuff like, "Does that school have a diving team?" and "I hear those mud baths are good for wrinkles."

24   Dad got up and snapped off the TV. The four of us sat there in stony silence.

---

1. **varsity ring** a ring given to a player on a school sports team

25 I was thinking that if I were at somebody else's house, we'd be rolling on the floor and laughing at this. I was thinking that kids all over Florida were rolling on the floor and laughing at this, at Erik Fisher the Flying Placekicker. But this isn't somebody else's house. This is the house built on the Erik Fisher Football Dream.

26 Finally Dad said to Erik, "Hey! All you can do is laugh it off."

27 Mom agreed. "That's right. You just leave it behind you. That's all you can do. You leave it behind you, and it's over with."

28 The four of us got up and went our separate ways—me up to my room.

29 I stared out my window at the back wall. *Forget it, Dad. Forget it, Mom. Erik can't laugh this off. Erik can't leave this humiliation behind him. Someone has to pay for this. I'm not sure* why *I'm sure. But I am. Someone has to pay for this.*

Excerpted from *Tangerine* by Edward Bloor, published by Houghton Mifflin Harcourt.

✏ WRITE

PERSONAL RESPONSE: Think about what makes someone a good teammate and why. Are the football players in this excerpt good teammates? Why or why not? Support your answer with examples from the text as well as your own experiences.

My Mother Really Knew

POETRY
Wing Tek Lum
1998

Introduction

The author of multiple collections, Wing Tek Lum (b. 1946) is a contemporary Hawaii-born American poet who uses his poetry as a conduit to explore the human condition. Through the exploration of individual moments and images, he draws lessons both universal and poignant. In the poem presented here, "My Mother Really Knew," Lum's reflection on a single memory illuminates the complex

"My father was a tough cookie, his friends still tell me with a smile."

NOTES

1 My father was a tough cookie,
2 his friends still tell me with a smile.
3 He was hot-tempered
4 and had to have his own way,
5 but they loved him **nonetheless,**
6 and so did I.

7 I remember that
8 for maybe the first decade[1] of my life
9 I had to kiss him every night
10 before I went to bed.

11 There was one time
12 he got into a big argument
13 with the rest of us at dinnertime,
14 and afterwards when he was in his study
15 I had to go to sleep
16 and refused to see him,
17 a chip off the old block.

18 But my mother and elder brothers
19 **coaxed** me to his door,
20 and I ran in
21 and pecked[2] his cheek
22 without saying a word,
23 and went to bed
24 thinking of how unfair life was.

---

1. **decade** a period of 10 years
2. **pecked** gave a short, gentle kiss

Please note that excerpts and passages in the StudySync® library and this workbook are intended as touchstones to generate interest in an author's work. The excerpts and passages do not substitute for the reading of entire texts, and StudySync® strongly recommends that students seek out and purchase the whole literary or informational work in order to experience it as the author intended. Links to online resellers are available in our digital library. In addition, complete works may be ordered through an authorized reseller by filling out and returning to StudySync® the order form enclosed in this workbook.

Reading & Writing Companion   **93**

NOTES

25 Love, my mother really knew,
26 was like these islands
27 formed in part
28 by tidal waves³ and hurricanes
29 and the **eruptions** of volcanoes,
30 which suddenly appear
31 and just as suddenly go away.

© 1988 by Wing Tek Lum, *Expounding the Doubtful Points*. Reproduced by permission of Wing Tek Lum.

---

3. **tidal wave** a very tall, strong wave that is sometimes dangerous

First Read

Read "My Mother Really Knew." After you read, complete the Think Questions below.

 THINK QUESTIONS

1. What is the thing that the speaker's mother knew? How does the author describe it? Cite evidence from the text in your response.

2. Why does the speaker refuse to see his father before going to bed? Be sure to include evidence from the text in your answer.

3. How do the first and last stanzas tell the lesson of the poem? Cite evidence from the text in your response.

4. In line 5, the speaker claims that his father's friends "loved him **nonetheless**." Based on context clues from the first stanza, what do you think the word *nonetheless* means? Write your definition here and identify clues that helped you figure out the meaning.

5. Look at the word *eruption* as it is used in the final stanza. Think of other instances in which you have heard the word *eruption*, as well as related words like *erupt*. Write a definition for *eruption* that includes the various uses.

Please note that excerpts and passages in the StudySync® library and this workbook are intended as touchstones to generate interest in an author's work. The excerpts and passages do not substitute for the reading of entire texts, and StudySync® strongly recommends that students seek out and purchase the whole literary or informational work in order to experience it as the author intended. Links to online resellers are available in our digital library. In addition, complete works may be ordered through an authorized reseller by filling out and returning to StudySync® the order form enclosed in this workbook.

Reading & Writing Companion   **95**

Skill:
Compare and Contrast

Use the Checklist to analyze Compare and Contrast in "My Mother Really Knew."

••• CHECKLIST FOR COMPARE AND CONTRAST

In order to compare and contrast texts within and across different forms and genres, do the following:

- ✓ choose two or more texts with similar subjects, topics, settings, or characters
- ✓ highlight evidence that reveals each text's theme or central message
  - • consider what happens as a result of the characters' words and actions
  - • note ways in which the texts are similar and different

To compare and contrast texts within and across different forms or genres, consider the following questions:

- ✓ What are the similarities and differences in the subjects or topics of the texts I have chosen?
- ✓ Have I looked at the words of each character, as well as what the characters do, to help me determine the theme of each work?

COMPARE AND CONTRAST
sync·skills

Skill:
Compare and Contrast

Reread lines 11–17 of "My Mother Really Knew," paragraph 10 of *Tangerine*, paragraphs 10–12 from *A Christmas Carol*, and the "Common Theme" comparison below. Then, complete the chart by matching the details that support the comparison with the correct text.

↻ YOUR TURN

COMMON THEME: Two people are at odds, and the conflict results in angry feelings and even insults.

Detail Options	
A	One person humiliates another
B	One person refuses to apologize after an argument
C	One person hurts another's feelings

"My Mother Really Knew"	Tangerine	A Christmas Carol

Please note that excerpts and passages in the StudySync® library and this workbook are intended as touchstones to generate interest in an author's work. The excerpts and passages do not substitute for the reading of entire texts, and StudySync® strongly recommends that students seek out and purchase the whole literary or informational work in order to experience it as the author intended. Links to online resellers are available in our digital library. In addition, complete works may be ordered through an authorized reseller by filling out and returning to StudySync® the order form enclosed in this workbook.

Reading & Writing Companion

97

Close Read

Reread "My Mother Really Knew." As you reread, complete the Skills Focus questions below. Then use your answers and annotations from the questions to help you complete the Write activity.

⊙ SKILLS FOCUS

1. Highlight examples of figurative language such as imagery or simile in "My Mother Really Knew." Choose one example and explain its meaning. Explain what the figurative language adds to the poem that plain language would not.

2. In *Tangerine*, the mother tries to convince her family to get out of the rain. Identify examples of the mother trying to convince her family in "My Mother Really Knew." Compare the ways in which the two mothers attempt to convince their families.

3. The character Scrooge in *A Christmas Carol* is mean and greedy. Identify a detail that shows which character in "My Mother Really Knew" is most similar to Scrooge. Explain how the characters are similar and different.

4. Identify the lessons that the speaker of "My Mother Really Knew" learns about love from his relationship with his parents and the loss of his father.

✏ WRITE

COMPARE AND CONTRAST: Compare and contrast the conflicts in the family interactions presented in "My Mother Really Knew" and the other two selections—*A Christmas Carol* and *Tangerine*. Remember to use evidence from all three texts to support your analysis.

Extended
Writing
Project and
Grammar

EXTENDED
WRITING
PROJECT
LITERARY ANALYSIS
WRITING

Literary Analysis Writing Process: Plan

PLAN	DRAFT	REVISE	EDIT AND PUBLISH

The authors in this unit all use their writing to explore important relationships. Many of these relationships, like Gavin's in "The Walking Dance," are complicated and difficult. Gavin struggles to feel a sense of belonging in his wife's family. But after attending a funeral service, Gavin finds a connection with them through the experience of love and loss.

WRITING PROMPT

What do we learn from love and loss?

Think about the main characters, narrators, or speakers in the texts from this unit. Choose two or three selections from the unit and write a literary analysis that shows the different types of lessons learned about love and loss. In your analysis, be sure to present an argument in which you explain what lesson each character, narrator, or speaker learns and how love or loss helps them learn this lesson. Be sure your literary analysis includes the following:

- an introduction
- a thesis statement with claims
- coherent body paragraphs
- reasons and evidence
- a conclusion

Writing to Sources

As you gather ideas and information from the texts, or sources, in the unit, be sure to:

- include a claim about each source;
- use evidence from each source; and
- avoid overly relying on one source.

Introduction to Argumentative Writing

An argumentative essay is a form of persuasive writing where the writer makes claim(s) about a topic and then provides evidence—facts, details, examples, and quotations—to convince readers to accept and agree with the writer's claim(s). In order to provide convincing supporting evidence for an argumentative essay, the writer must often do outside research as well as cite the sources of the evidence that is presented. In an essay, a thesis statement usually appears at the end of the introductory paragraph and offers a concise summary of the claim.

A literary analysis is a form of argumentative writing that tries to persuade readers to accept the writer's interpretation of a literary text. Good literary analysis writing builds an argument with claims, convincing reasons, relevant textual evidence, and a clear structure with an introduction with a thesis statement, body paragraphs, and a conclusion. The characteristics of argumentative writing include:

- introduction
- thesis statement
- claims
- textual evidence
- transitions
- formal style
- conclusion

As you continue with this Extended Writing Project, you'll receive more instruction and practice at crafting each of the characteristics of argumentative writing to create your own literary analysis.

Before you get started on your own literary analysis, read this literary analysis that one student, Knox, wrote in response to the writing prompt. As you read the Model, highlight and annotate the features of argumentative writing that Knox included in his literary analysis.

☰ STUDENT MODEL

Lessons from Love and Loss

1   Relationships have highs and lows. In many cases, relationships are the best thing in life. Other times, relationships are full of conflict. In literature, authors express lessons about love and loss by exploring deep relationships. For example, "My Mother Pieced Quilts" conveys that family and relationships are a combination of both love and loss; a family's history has moments of joy and of pain, but through it all, they are rooted in love. In a similar way, "The Walking Dance" shows that people find their roles in family relationships. "Annabel Lee" reveals that the power of love and loss in relationships can make people unreasonable. The authors of these three texts express in different ways that love and loss teach people about themselves and their relationships.

2   The speaker in "My Mother Pieced Quilts" learns that families move forward together by working together, supporting each other, and loving each other in good times and bad. The speaker watches her mother quilt and writes about "black silk" at "grandmother's/funeral" and the "lilac purple of easter." This shows the pieces of fabric represent both happy and sad memories and all different times and places throughout their family history. The speaker describes the quilts like family members who love and support each other. The quilts are "armed/ready/shouting/celebrating" and "sing on" despite a past of "laughing and sobbing." This shows that the speaker learns loss and tough times are easier when families work together and love each other. The speaker also remembers how these quilts protected her family from the cold, just like families protect each other when times are hard. For example, the speaker talks about how her mother "stretched and turned and re-arranged" fabric to make a quilt. This is just like how parents stretch their resources and make sacrifices to keep their children safe. Overall, it is clear that the speaker learns the importance of loving, supporting, and working with your family.

3 Like the speaker in "My Mother Pieced Quilts," the character Gavin in "The Walking Dance" learns that family relationships take work. Gavin is visiting his wife Aurora's family in San Antonio. Gavin feels like an outsider in the big Herrera family, who tease and ignore him at times. He feels alone at the funeral of Aurora's aunt Melchora. He's only an accessory to Aurora: "If something happened to Aurora, he'd be swallowed up by her mammoth family, totally invisible. Barely anyone would know him." But then grief overcomes Gavin's son Carlos, and he needs his father. Gavin picks up Carlos from his grandmother's arms and joins the ceremonial walking dance with his family. "He lifted Carlos out of Cookie's arms. This kiddo was heavy, but Gavin could tough it out for at least one lap around the chapel with his mother-in-law." They share a moment. Cookie sums it up, "That's right. Let's go." Though his family relationships are not perfect, Gavin learns how to connect with his family members through love and loss.

4 The poem "Annabel Lee" takes a darker turn because Edgar Allan Poe explores the irrational thoughts of a speaker mourning his departed love. The speaker's love for Annabel Lee is so powerful that he believes it makes angels jealous: "The angels, not half so happy in Heaven, / Went envying her and me—." The speaker shows extreme devotion to his relationship, even after the death of Annabel Lee. "And neither the angels in Heaven above / Nor the demons down under the sea / Can ever dissever my soul from the soul / Of the beautiful Annabel Lee." This poetic statement shows that the speaker does not move on from Annabel Lee after losing her. He also holds on to the relationship to make it everlasting. "For the moon never beams, without bringing me dreams / Of the beautiful Annabel Lee." The speaker expresses that deep relationships of love can extend beyond any loss, which includes the profound loss of death. The speaker learns that he cannot move on without Annabel Lee, so his love dominates his thoughts.

5 "My Mother Pieced Quilts," "The Walking Dance," and "Annabel Lee" show how speakers and characters learn about themselves through the challenges of love and loss. The speaker in "My Mother Pieced Quilts" remembers both the highs and lows of her childhood and family history, but through it all is surrounded by love and support. Gavin in "The Walking Dance" learns how to contribute to his family

Please note that excerpts and passages in the StudySync® library and this workbook are intended as touchstones to generate interest in an author's work. The excerpts and passages do not substitute for the reading of entire texts, and StudySync® strongly recommends that students seek out and purchase the whole literary or informational work in order to experience it as the author intended. Links to online resellers are available in our digital library. In addition, complete works may be ordered through an authorized reseller by filling out and returning to StudySync® the order form enclosed in this workbook.

Reading & Writing Companion   103

NOTES

through his son's grief. The speaker in "Annabel Lee" learns that his feelings for his lost love overwhelm him. The characters and speakers in these selections focus on their deepest relationships. They make sure they do not fade. This helps the speaker in "My Mother Pieced Quilts" and the character Gavin in "The Walking Dance" stay close with their families. On the other hand, this quality makes it hard for the speaker in "Annabel Lee" to carry on when he loses his love, but he chooses that path. By dealing with love and loss, the characters and speakers learn about their own place in the world.

WRITE

Writers often take notes before they sit down to write. Think about what you've learned so far about literary analyses to help you begin prewriting.

- Which texts from the unit would you like to write about?

- How do the characters, narrators, or speakers of those texts express their ideas about love and loss?

- What kinds of lessons do the characters, speakers, or narrators learn?

- What kinds of textual evidence might you use to support your ideas?

- What kinds of transitional words and phrases could you use to connect your ideas in a logical way?

Response Instructions

Use the questions in the bulleted list to write a one-paragraph summary. Your summary should identify the two or three texts you want to write about. Explain how the characters, narrators, or speakers of each of those texts learn a lesson.

Don't worry about including all of the details now; focus only on the most essential and important elements. You will refer back to this short paragraph as you continue through the steps of the writing process.

Please note that excerpts and passages in the StudySync® library and this workbook are intended as touchstones to generate interest in an author's work. The excerpts and passages do not substitute for the reading of entire texts, and StudySync® strongly recommends that students seek out and purchase the whole literary or informational work in order to experience it as the author intended. Links to online resellers are available in our digital library. In addition, complete works may be ordered through an authorized reseller by filling out and returning to StudySync® the order form enclosed in this workbook.

Reading & Writing Companion **105**

Skill:
Thesis Statement

••• CHECKLIST FOR THESIS STATEMENT

Before you begin writing your thesis statement, ask yourself the following questions:

- What is the prompt asking me to write about?
- What is the topic of my essay? How can I state it clearly for the reader?
- What claim(s) do I want to make about the topic of this essay? Is my opinion clear to my reader?

Here are some methods to introduce and develop your thesis statement clearly:

- Think about the prompt topic.
  - > Read the prompt topic closely.
  - > Identify keywords or questions in the prompt.

- Select and review your selections to solidify your thesis statement.
  - > Select the two or three texts to use.
  - > Think about or take notes on the main ideas of each text.
  - > Find connections between the main ideas of each text.

- Write a clear statement about the central idea or thesis statement.
  - > Let the reader anticipate the body of your essay.
  - > Respond completely to the writing prompt.

YOUR TURN

Complete the chart by matching the student action with the correct step of writing a thesis statement.

	Student Action Options
A	Mike picks the two texts he will use and rereads them, taking notes on the main ideas of each text and how they connect to the topic of his essay. Mike rereads his notes on both the prompt and the text selections. He notices that all of the characters in the different texts persevered through different challenges and were eventually successful.
B	Mike continues to review his notes. Then, he provides a one-sentence summary of his main points: "The characters in these two texts show that challenges and adversity can make you stronger."
C	Mike rereads and highlights keywords in the writing prompt so that he knows what the topic of his essay should be about. He notes that in his essay he will need to analyze how characters react to challenges and adversity in at least two different texts.

Steps to Writing an Effective Thesis Statement	Student Actions
Think about the prompt topic.	
Select and review your selections to solidify your claims.	
Write a clear thesis statement.	

✏ WRITE

Follow the steps in the checklist section to draft a thesis statement for your literary analysis.

Skill: Organizing Argumentative Writing

••• CHECKLIST FOR ORGANIZING ARGUMENTATIVE WRITING

As you consider how to organize your writing for your literary analysis, use the following questions as a guide:

- What is my thesis statement? What claim about each text supports my thesis statement?

- Have I chosen the best organizational structure to present my information logically?

- Can my claims be supported by logical reasoning and relevant evidence?

- Do I have enough evidence to support my thesis statement and claims?

Follow these steps to plan out the organization of your literary analysis, including organizing your reasons and evidence logically:

- Identify and write your thesis statement and claims.

- Choose an organizational structure that will present your claims logically.

- Identify reasons and evidence that support each claim.

- Organize your ideas using an outline or graphic organizer.

YOUR TURN

Read the thesis and claim statements below. Then, complete the chart by matching each statement with its correct place in the outline.

	Thesis Statement and Claim Options
A	In these three works of fiction, the authors use conflict to show readers that people should be valued for the traits that make them unique.
B	The conflict between the cruel lord and the aging mother in "The Wise Old Woman" teaches that elderly people should be valued for their experience and that we all need to rely on each other.
C	After a conflict in the street, it may seem strange that Mrs. Jones invites Roger into her home in "Thank You, Ma'am."
D	In conclusion, through various conflicts, the authors of these three texts were able to show that different traits make us unique and should be valued.
E	There is no one else quite like Stargirl in Jerry Spinelli's novel—other students don't fully understand her, but that's what makes Stargirl special.

Outline	Thesis Statement or Claim
Thesis Statement	
Claim 1: "Wise Old Woman"	
Claim 2: *Stargirl*	
Claim 3: "Thank You, Ma'am"	
Restate Thesis Statement	

YOUR TURN

Complete the chart below by writing your thesis statement and claim for each body paragraph. Repeat your thesis statement for your conclusion.

Outline	Thesis Statement or Claim
Thesis Statement	
Claim 1	
Claim 2	
Claim 3	
Restate Thesis Statement	

Skill: Reasons and Relevant Evidence

As you begin to determine what reasons and relevant evidence will support your claim(s), use the following questions as a guide:

• What is the claim (or claims) that I am making in my argument?

• What textual evidence am I using to support this claim? Is it relevant?

• Am I quoting the source accurately?

• Does my evidence display logical reasoning and relate to the claim I am making?

Use the following steps as a guide to help you determine how you will support your claim(s) with logical reasoning and relevant evidence, using accurate and credible sources:

• Identify the claim(s) you will make in your argument.

• Select evidence from credible sources that will convince others to accept your claim(s).

• Explain the connection between your claim(s) and the evidence and ensure your reasoning is logical, develops naturally from the evidence, and supports your claim.

Please note that excerpts and passages in the StudySync® library and this workbook are intended as touchstones to generate interest in an author's work. The excerpts and passages do not substitute for the reading of entire texts, and StudySync® strongly recommends that students seek out and purchase the whole literary or informational work in order to experience it as the author intended. Links to online resellers are available in our digital library. In addition, complete works may be ordered through an authorized reseller by filling out and returning to StudySync® the order form enclosed in this workbook.

Reading & Writing Companion

111

↻ YOUR TURN

Read each piece of textual evidence below. Then, complete the chart by deciding which evidence best supports each claim and explain how the evidence supports the claim. The first row has been done for you.

Evidence Options	
A	For example, young viewers learn that those who treat others with pettiness and contempt become rich and famous. In fact, in 2011, one of the stars of *Jersey Shore* was paid more to address Rutgers University students than was Toni Morrison, a Nobel prize–winning author.
B	Today, according to the *Asbury Park Press*, each New Jersey school district spends more than thirty thousand dollars a year devoted to anti-bullying measures.
C	Programs such as *Project Runway*, *The Voice*, and *So You Think You Can Dance* give artists and performers a chance to appear before millions to show their talents.

Claim	Evidence	Explanation
Schools are not doing enough to prevent bullying.	The National Center for Education Statistics reported in 2013 that one of three students is bullied either in school or through social media.	This supports the idea that many students are being bullied and schools are not doing enough.
Most schools are doing their best to stop bullying.		
Reality television is harmful.		
Reality television can be positive.		

⟳ YOUR TURN

Complete the chart below by writing a piece of evidence that supports each claim and explain how the evidence supports the claim.

Claim	Evidence	Explanation
Claim for Selection #1		
Claim for Selection #2		
Claim for Selection #3		

Literary Analysis Writing Process: Draft

PLAN	DRAFT	REVISE	EDIT AND PUBLISH

You have already made progress toward writing your literary analysis. Now it is time to draft your literary analysis.

✏ WRITE

Use your plan and other responses in your Binder to draft your literary analysis. You may also have new ideas as you begin drafting. Feel free to explore any new ideas. You can also ask yourself these questions:

- Is my thesis statement clear?
- Is my textual evidence relevant and necessary?
- Does the organizational structure make sense?

Before you submit your draft, read it over carefully. You want to be sure that you've responded to all aspects of the prompt.

Here is Knox's literary analysis. As you read, identify relevant textual evidence that develops his thesis. Because this is a draft, there are some errors that Knox will revise as he works toward his final version.

☰ STUDENT MODEL: FIRST DRAFT

Lessons from Love and Loss

~~In literature authors explore lessons about life by exploring relationships. The authors of these three texts showed in different ways that the rewards of deep relationships require effort. The relationships in "My Mother Pieced Quilts," "Walking Dance," and "Annabel Lee" show that people have to work at relationships to maintain and improve them, but no one can make them perfect. These three literary texts show in diverse ways how love and loss teach us that it is important to move forward.~~

Relationships have highs and lows. In many cases, relationships are the best thing in life. Other times, relationships are full of conflict. In literature, authors express lessons about love and loss by exploring deep relationships. For example, "My Mother Pieced Quilts" conveys that family and relationships are a combination of both love and loss; a family's history has moments of joy and of pain, but through it all, they are rooted in love. In a similar way, "The Walking Dance" shows that people find their roles in family relationships. "Annabel Lee" reveals that the power of love and loss in relationships can make people unreasonable. The authors of these three texts express in different ways that love and loss teach people about themselves and their relationships.

The speaker in "My Mother Pieced Quilts" learns that families move forward together and support each other through good times and bad. The speaker watches her mother quilt and writes about "black silk" at "grandmother's/funeral" and the "lilac purple of easter." This shows the pieces of fabric represent both happy and sad memories and all different times and places throughout their family history. The speaker describes the quilts like family members who love and support each other. The quilts are "armed/ready/shouting/celebrating" and "sing on" despite a past of "laughing and sobbing." This shows that the speaker learns loss and tough times are easier when families work together and love each other. This poem shows that even though bad things happened, she still loved her family and had good memories.

Skill:
Introductions

Knox added several sentences in the beginning of his introductory paragraph to grab his readers' attention. Then, he introduced them to the topic from the prompt, love and loss. Finally, he revised his thesis statement to clarify that the characters in each text learned about themselves and their relationships. He placed his thesis statement last in the introduction.

NOTES

Skill:
Transitions

Knox realizes that he is missing some transitions in this body paragraph. He realizes this paragraph does not logically follow the previous one. He decides to add a stronger topic sentence that introduces his main idea to relate it to the previous paragraph about "My Mother Pieced Quilts." He also decides to add some transitions to better connect his ideas.

~~The short story explores being an outsider to a group. Gavin is visiting his wife Aurora's family in San Antonio. He feels like an outsider in the big Herrera family. Especially at the funeral of Aurora's aunt Melchora. It's as if he's only an accessory to Aurora: "If something happened to Aurora, he'd be swallowed up by her mammoth family, totally invisible. Barely anyone would know him." Grief overcomes Gavin's son Carlos, and he needs his father. Though his family relationships are not perfect, Gavin learns.~~

Like the speaker in "My Mother Pieced Quilts," the character Gavin in "The Walking Dance" learns that family relationships take work. Gavin is visiting his wife Aurora's family in San Antonio. Gavin feels like an outsider in the big Herrera family, who tease and ignore him at times. He feels alone at the funeral of Aurora's aunt Melchora. He's only an accessory to Aurora: "If something happened to Aurora, he'd be swallowed up by her mammoth family, totally invisible. Barely anyone would know him." **But then** grief overcomes Gavin's son Carlos, and he needs his father. Gavin picks up Carlos from his grandmother's arms and joins the ceremonial walking dance with his family. "He lifted Carlos out of Cookie's arms. This kiddo was heavy, but Gavin could tough it out for at least one lap around the chapel with his mother-in-law." They share a moment. Cookie sums it up, "That's right. Let's go." **Though** his family relationships are not perfect, Gavin learns how to connect with his family members through love and loss.

~~The text takes a darker turn and showed how the speaker's focus on a relationship makes him irrational. The thoughts of a speaker mourning his departed love. The speaker's love for Annabel Lee is so powerful that he believes it makes angels jealous. The speaker shows extreme devotion to his relationship even continues after the death of Annabe lee. This poetic statement shows that the speaker does not move on from Annabel Lee after losing her, and he holds onto the relationship to make it everlasting. "For the moon never beams, without bringing me dreams / Of the beautiful Annabel Lee." The speaker expresses that deep relationships of love can extend beyond any loss which includes the profound loss of death. I~~

~~learned that he cannot move on without Annabel Lee, so his love~~
~~dominates his thoughts.~~

The poem "Annabel Lee" takes a darker turn because Edgar Allan Poe explores the irrational thoughts of a speaker mourning his departed love. The speaker's love for Annabel Lee is so powerful that he believes it makes angels jealous. "The angels, not half so happy in Heaven, / Went envying her and me—." The speaker shows extreme devotion to his relationship, even after the death of Annabel Lee. "And neither the angels in Heaven above / Nor the demons down under the sea / Can ever dissever my soul from the soul / Of the beautiful Annabel Lee." This poetic statement shows that the speaker does not move on from Annabel Lee after losing her. He also holds on to the relationship to make it everlasting. "For the moon never beams, without bringing me dreams / Of the beautiful Annabel Lee." The speaker expresses that deep relationships of love can extend beyond any loss, which includes the profound loss of death. The speaker learns that he cannot move on without Annabel Lee, so his love dominates his thoughts.

~~"My Mother Pieced Quilts," "The Walking Dance," and "Annabel Lee"~~
~~show that hardships occur even in the strongest relationships. "My~~
~~Mother Pieced Quilts" shows the upside and downside of family~~
~~relationships. "Walking Dance" shows how family relationships come~~
~~together in difficult times. The relationship described in "Annabel~~
~~Lee" shows the power of love. The speakers and characters do the~~
~~best they can in these situations and try to move forward. They react~~
~~to their situations and make their relationships a priority. Otherwise,~~
~~their relationships would fade away.~~

"My Mother Pieced Quilts," "The Walking Dance," and "Annabel Lee" show how speakers and characters learn about themselves through the challenges of love and loss. The speaker in "My Mother Pieced Quilts" remembers both the highs and lows of her childhood and family history, but through it all is surrounded by love and support. Gavin in "The Walking Dance" learns how to contribute to his family through his son's grief. The speaker in "Annabel Lee" learns that his

Skill:
Style

Knox changes his first sentence to include more academic language (specifying "poem" and the title) and establish an academic tone. He continues to maintain that tone by replacing the first person (I) in the last sentence.

Please note that excerpts and passages in the StudySync® library and this workbook are intended as touchstones to generate interest in an author's work. The excerpts and passages do not substitute for the reading of entire texts, and StudySync® strongly recommends that students seek out and purchase the whole literary or informational work in order to experience it as the author intended. Links to online resellers are available in our digital library. In addition, complete works may be ordered through an authorized reseller by filling out and returning to StudySync® the order form enclosed in this workbook.

Reading & Writing
Companion

117

NOTES

Skill:
Conclusions

Knox begins his conclusion by restating his thesis statement a new way. He chose to highlight all three texts and how they taught lessons through love and loss. By repeating his thesis statement one more time, he highlighted the common lesson that all the speakers and characters learned.

feelings for his lost love overwhelm him. The characters and speakers in these selections focus on their deepest relationships. They make sure they do not fade. This helps the speaker in "My Mother Pieced Quilts" and the character Gavin in "The Walking Dance" stay close with their families. On the other hand, this quality makes it hard for the speaker in "Annabel Lee" to carry on when he loses his love, but he chooses that path. By dealing with love and loss, the characters and speakers learn about their own place in the world.

Skill:
Introductions

••• CHECKLIST FOR INTRODUCTIONS

Before you write your introduction, ask yourself the following questions:

- What is my thesis statement?
- How can I introduce my topic clearly?
- How can I preview my selections?
- How can I "hook" readers' interest?
    - > Start with an attention-grabbing statement.
    - > Begin with an intriguing question.
    - > Use descriptive words to set a scene.

Below are two strategies to help you write a clear and engaging introduction:

- Peer Discussion
    - > Talk about your topic with a partner, explaining what you already know and your ideas about your topic.
    - > Write notes about the ideas you have discussed and any new questions you may have.
    - > Review your notes and think about what will be your thesis statement.
    - > Briefly state your thesis statement.
    - > Write a sentence to introduce the topic.
    - > Write ways you can give readers a "preview" of what they will read in the rest of your essay.
    - > Write a possible "hook."

- Freewriting
    - > Freewrite for ten minutes about your topic. Don't worry about grammar, punctuation, or having fully formed ideas. The point of freewriting is to discover ideas.
    - > Review your notes and think about what will be your thesis statement.
    - > Briefly state your thesis statement.
    - > Write a sentence to introduce the topic.
    - > Write ways you can give readers a "preview" of what they will read in the rest of your essay.
    - > Write a possible "hook."

Please note that excerpts and passages in the StudySync® library and this workbook are intended as touchstones to generate interest in an author's work. The excerpts and passages do not substitute for the reading of entire texts, and StudySync® strongly recommends that students seek out and purchase the whole literary or informational work in order to experience it as the author intended. Links to online resellers are available in our digital library. In addition, complete works may be ordered through an authorized reseller by filling out and returning to StudySync® the order form enclosed in this workbook.

Reading & Writing Companion **119**

YOUR TURN

Read each response from Knox's partner below. Then, match each response to the correct section of the introduction.

	Response Options
A	We all understand love and loss, and authors use our understanding of love and loss to teach us important lessons.
B	Aren't relationships the best and the worst at the same time? They can make you happy and feel loved, but they can also make you feel sad and alone.
C	In all three of these texts, the authors used the speakers to show how love and loss can help us find ourselves.
D	In the poem "Annabel Lee," the speaker loved deeply, but then struggled when they lost the person they loved. In "The Walking Dance," the speaker struggled to find their place in their family; even though they were surrounded by love, it took a loss for them to step up. Finally, in "My Mother Pieced Quilts," the speakers explored how family relationships are made up of many moments of joy and sadness and that the love helps them find themselves and keeps them grounded.

Part of Introduction	Response
Hook	
Introduce topic	
Preview	
Clear thesis statement	

✏ WRITE

Use the steps in the checklist section to revise the introduction of your literary analysis essay.

Skill:
Transitions

••• CHECKLIST FOR TRANSITIONS

Before you revise your current draft to include transitions, think about:

- the key ideas you discuss in your body paragraphs
- how your paragraphs connect together to support your claim(s)
- the relationships among your claim(s), reasons, and evidence

Next, reread your current draft and note areas in your essay where:

- the relationships between your claim(s) and the reasons and evidence are unclear, identifying places where you could add linking words or other transitional devices to make your argument more cohesive. Look for:

  > sudden jumps in your ideas

  > breaks between paragraphs where the ideas in the next paragraph are not logically following from the previous one

Revise your draft to use words, phrases, and clauses to create cohesion and clarify the relationships among claim(s) and reasons, using the following questions as a guide:

- Are there unifying relationships between the claims, reasons, and evidence I present in my argument?
- Have I clarified, or made clear, these relationships?
- What linking words (such as conjunctions), phrases, or clauses could I add to my argument to clarify the relationships between the claims, reasons, and evidence I present?

YOUR TURN

Choose the best answer to each question.

1. The following section is from an earlier draft of Knox's essay. Knox has not used the most effective transition in the underlined sentence. Which of the following could he add to the underlined sentence?

> The speaker expresses that deep relationships of love can extend beyond any loss, which includes the profound loss of death. <u>He learns that he cannot move on without Annabel Lee, so his love dominates his thoughts.</u>

○ A. For instance,

○ B. Equally important,

○ C. Finally,

○ D. Similarly,

2. The following section is from an earlier draft of Knox's essay. He would like to add a sentence to bring this paragraph to a more effective close. Which sentence could he add after sentence 5 to help achieve this goal?

> (1) In "My Mother Pieced Quilts," the speaker remembers all the different stuff her family did. (2) The speaker remembers how the quilts protected them from the cold and showed her family history. (3) The speaker talks about how her mom sewed all different pieces and parts into the quilt and they protected everyone from the cold. (4) Her mom used all different things for the quilts; she says her mom used pieces that showed "your michigan spring faded curtain pieces / my father's santa fe work shirt / the summer denims, the tweed of fall." (5) She talked about the quilts showing all the family history, good and bad.

○ A. Throughout this poem, the speaker realizes that even though her family suffered loss, they were still surrounded by love, and the memories of both were important.

○ B. The speaker misses her family, especially her mother.

○ C. For example, the speaker would like to remember the good and bad parts of her family history.

○ D. I think the speaker is a kind person for remembering her family with love.

⟳ YOUR TURN

Complete the chart by writing a transitional sentence below the example that connects ideas with or between paragraphs in your essay.

Purpose	Example and Your Sentence
add information	**In addition**, it is important to remember that female athletes play as many or more games a season than male athletes.
introduce examples	**For example**, the New York Liberty and the Washington Mystics both play 15 more games a season than the New York Knicks and the Washington Wizards.
discuss a contradiction	**Even though** they are working more hours, attending more practices, and playing more games a season, women are being paid less; this may be because there are fewer fans watching and attending their games.
show time sequence	**At this time**, this is changing; female athletes like Hope Solo and Serena Williams are beginning to draw attention to the gender discrepancies in professional sports.
show cause and effect	**As a result**, more people are paying attention to the conditions, pay, and treatment of female athletes.
summarize	**In summary**, I believe it is important that we acknowledge that female professional athletes are working just as hard as their male counterparts and deserve to be recognized for that work.

Skill:
Style

sync•skills

••• CHECKLIST FOR STYLE

First, reread the draft of your argumentative essay and identify the following:

- places where you use slang, contractions, abbreviations, and a conversational tone

- areas where you could use subject-specific or academic language in order to help, persuade, or inform your readers

- moments where you use first person (*I*) or second person (*you*)

- areas where sentence structure lacks variety

- incorrect uses of the conventions of standard English for grammar, spelling, capitalization, and punctuation

Establish and maintain a formal style in your essay, using the following questions as a guide:

- Have I avoided slang in favor of academic language?

- Did I consistently use a third-person point of view, using third-person pronouns (*he*, *she*, *they*)?

- Have I varied my sentence structure and the length of my sentences? Apply these specific questions where appropriate:

  > Where should I make some sentences longer by using conjunctions to connect independent clauses, dependent clauses, and phrases?

  > Where should I make some sentences shorter by separating any independent clauses?

- Did I follow the conventions of standard English, including:

  > grammar?

  > spelling?

  > capitalization?

  > punctuation?

⟳ YOUR TURN

Complete the chart below by correcting each piece of informal language with the formal language.

Formal/Academic Language Options			
should not	was not	they/she/he (third person)	television
the reader	did not	text	want to

Informal Language	Formal/Academic Language
didn't	
story	
shouldn't	
wanna	
wasn't	
I/me/we (first person)	
you	
TV	

YOUR TURN

Complete the chart by identifying parts of your essay that may need to be rewritten in a more formal style.

Common Informal Language	Rewrite
Contractions	
First Person	
Slang	
Conversational Tone	

Skill:
Conclusions

Before you write your conclusion, ask yourself the following questions:

- How can I restate the thesis statement in my concluding section? What impression can I make on my reader?

- How can I write my conclusion so that it supports and follows logically from my argument?

- Should I include a call to action?

- How can I conclude with a memorable comment?

Below are two strategies to help you provide a concluding statement or section that follows from and supports the argument presented:

- Peer Discussion

  > After you have written your introduction and body paragraphs, talk with a partner and tell him or her what you want readers to remember, writing notes about your discussion.

  > Review your notes and think about what you wish to express in your conclusion.

  > Rewrite your thesis statement in a different way.

  > Briefly review and explain how your claims about each selection support your thesis.

  > Include a call to action or memorable comment at the end.

  > Write your conclusion.

- Freewriting

  > Freewrite for ten minutes about what you might include in your conclusion. Don't worry about grammar, punctuation, or having fully formed ideas. The point of freewriting is to discover ideas.

  > Review your notes and think about what you wish to express in your conclusion.

  > Rewrite your thesis statement in a different way.

  > Briefly review and explain how your claims about each selection support your thesis.

  > Include a call to action or memorable comment at the end.

  > Write your conclusion.

Please note that excerpts and passages in the StudySync® library and this workbook are intended as touchstones to generate interest in an author's work. The excerpts and passages do not substitute for the reading of entire texts, and StudySync® strongly recommends that students seek out and purchase the whole literary or informational work in order to experience it as the author intended. Links to online resellers are available in our digital library. In addition, complete works may be ordered through an authorized reseller by filling out and returning to StudySync® the order form enclosed in this workbook.

Reading & Writing
Companion

127

⟳ YOUR TURN

Read each response from Knox's partner below. Then, match each response to the correct section of the conclusion.

Response Options	
A	In the three texts, "Annabel Lee," "The Walking Dance," and "My Mother Pieced Quilts," the characters and speakers show how love and loss taught them lessons about themselves.
B	The authors show us that as human beings, we share these powerful feelings. We also learn so much from them.
C	In both "The Walking Dance" and the poem "Annabel Lee," Gavin and the speaker learn about themselves through the loss of someone dear to them. Gavin learns how important he is to his family and the speaker in "Annabel Lee" learns that he can persevere through the loss of his love. In the poem "My Mother Pieced Quilts," the speaker uses quilts to help her remember a family history that was filled with both love and loss.

Part of Conclusion	Response
Restate thesis statement in a different way	
Review and explain your claims	
Call to action or memorable comment	

✎ WRITE

Use the steps in the checklist section to revise the conclusion of your literary analysis essay.

Literary Analysis Writing Process: Revise

PLAN	DRAFT	REVISE	EDIT AND PUBLISH

You have written a draft of your literary analysis. You have also received input from your peers about how to improve it. Now you are going to revise your draft.

◀ REVISION GUIDE

Examine your draft to find areas for revision. Keep in mind your purpose and audience as you revise for clarity, development, organization, and style. Use the guide below to help you review:

Review	Revise	Example
Clarity		
Review your preview statement in your introduction. Identify any sentences where it is not clear which selection you are discussing.	Identify the title, author, speaker or narrator, and names of characters. Provide descriptions so readers understand your statements. Check that these same names and titles are also used throughout body paragraphs and your conclusion.	The poem "Annabel Lee" takes a darker turn and shows how the speaker's focus on the loss of his love makes him irrational.
Development		
Review the development of your claim in the body paragraphs. Identify statements that lack supporting evidence.	Check off each statement that is supported with textual evidence. Add quotations to follow statements that need support.	The speaker's love for Annabel Lee is so powerful that he believes it makes angels jealous: "The angels, not half so happy in Heaven, / Went envying her and me—." The speaker shows extreme devotion to his relationship, so it even continues after the death of Annabel Lee.

Review	Revise	Example
Organization		
Find places where transitions would improve your essay. Review your body paragraphs to identify and annotate any sentences that don't flow in a clear and logical way.	Rewrite the sentences so they appear in a logical sequence, starting with a clear transition or topic sentence. Delete details that are repetitive or not essential to support the thesis.	Like the speaker in "My Mother Pieced Quilts," the character Gavin in "The Walking Dance" learns that family relationships take work.
Style: Word Choice		
Identify sentences that refer to literary concepts. Look for everyday words and phrases that can be replaced with literary terms.	Replace everyday language with literary terms, such as *speaker*, *poem*, and *conflict*.	~~He~~ The speaker learns that he cannot move on without Annabel Lee, so his love dominates his thoughts.
Style: Sentence Variety		
Read your literary analysis aloud. Annotate places where you have too many long or short sentences in a row.	Rewrite sentences by making them longer or shorter for clarity or emphasis.	This poetic statement shows that the speaker does not move on from Annabel Lee after losing her. ~~, and he~~ He holds on to the relationship to make it everlasting.

✏ **WRITE**

Use the guide above, as well as your peer reviews, to help you evaluate your literary analysis to determine areas that should be revised.

Grammar: Adjective Clauses

A clause is a group of words that has a subject and a predicate. An adjective clause is a subordinate clause that modifies, or describes, a noun or pronoun. It answers the questions *who, what kind*, or *which one*? Many adjective clauses begin with a relative pronoun, including *that, which, who, whom*, or *whose*. Adjective clauses may also begin with *where* or *when*.

Sentence	Noun or Pronoun	Adjective Clause
It was a big change from my **mother who always lets out a screech** if you go near anything... *The Pigman*	mother	who always lets out a screech
His left leg was cut off close by the hip, and under the left shoulder, he carried a **crutch, which he managed with wonderful dexterity,** hopping about upon it like a bird. *Treasure Island*	crutch	which he managed with wonderful dexterity

⟳ YOUR TURN

1. Choose the revision that uses an adjective clause to modify a noun.

> Christopher drove his mother's car.

- ○ A. Christopher, a young boy, drove his mother's car.
- ○ B. Christopher, who did not have a license, drove his mother's car.
- ○ C. Christopher drove his mother's brand new car.
- ○ D. None of the above

2. Choose the revision that uses an adjective clause to modify a noun.

> Jack's kite looked like a giant caterpillar.

- ○ A. Jack's kite looked like a giant caterpillar that crept across the clouds.
- ○ B. Jack's kite, a box-like contraption, looked like a giant caterpillar.
- ○ C. Jack's kite looked like a giant, creeping caterpillar.
- ○ D. None of the above

3. Choose the revision that uses an adjective clause to modify a noun.

> Umberto forgot his umbrella at the restaurant.

- ○ A. When he got up to leave, Umberto forgot his umbrella at the restaurant.
- ○ B. Umberto, a careful man, forgot his umbrella at the restaurant.
- ○ C. Umberto, who usually never forgets, forgot his umbrella at the restaurant.
- ○ D. None of the above

4. Choose the revision that uses an adjective clause to modify a noun.

> Helen left her nephew in the care of her grandmother.

- ○ A. Helen, who was running late, left her nephew in the care of her grandmother.
- ○ B. Helen left her cute little nephew in the care of her grandmother.
- ○ C. Helen left her nephew in the care of her grandmother because she had no one else to watch him.
- ○ D. None of the above.

Grammar: Noun Clauses

A clause is a group of words that contains both a subject and a verb. A noun clause is a subordinate clause that acts as a noun in a sentence.

A noun clause usually begins with one of these words: *how, that, what, whatever, when, where, which, whichever, who, whom, whoever, whose,* or *why.*

Noun as Subject	Noun Clause as Subject
The **goalie** should get the MVP award.	**Whoever stopped that last goal attempt** should get the MVP award.

In most sentences containing noun clauses, you can replace the noun clause with a pronoun such as *he* or *it,* and the sentence will still make sense. You can use a noun clause in the same ways you use a noun—as a subject, a direct object, an indirect object, an object of a preposition, and a predicate noun.

Function of Clause	Text
Object of a Preposition	The woman did not ask the boy anything about **where he lived,** his folks, or anything else that would embarrass him. "Thank You, Ma'am"
Direct Object	The woman didn't know **where he lived.**
Subject	**Where he lived** wasn't important to the woman.
Predicate Noun	Quietly listening was **how she found out all she wanted to know.**

Please note that excerpts and passages in the StudySync® library and this workbook are intended as touchstones to generate interest in an author's work. The excerpts and passages do not substitute for the reading of entire texts, and StudySync® strongly recommends that students seek out and purchase the whole literary or informational work in order to experience it as the author intended. Links to online resellers are available in our digital library. In addition, complete works may be ordered through an authorized reseller by filling out and returning to StudySync® the order form enclosed in this workbook.

Reading & Writing Companion   **133**

YOUR TURN

1. Replace the word in bold with a noun clause.

> Your athletic skills will be valuable in **hockey**.

- ○ A. football, baseball, or tennis
- ○ B. any preferred sport
- ○ C. whichever sport you choose
- ○ D. No change needs to be made to this sentence.

2. Replace the words in bold with a noun clause.

> This is **how students select their major.**

- ○ A. the appropriate major
- ○ B. a difficult selection process
- ○ C. about students and their majors
- ○ D. No change needs to be made to this sentence.

3. Replace the words in bold with a noun clause.

> Choir directors seek **the person with the best voice**.

- ○ A. whoever has the best voice
- ○ B. those with great voices
- ○ C. soloists and chorus members
- ○ D. No change needs to be made to this sentence.

4. Replace the words in bold with a noun clause.

> **Reaching the next grade level** depends upon your study habits.

- ○ A. Advancement to the next grade level
- ○ B. When you reach the next grade level
- ○ C. Moving forward a grade level
- ○ D. No change needs to be made to this sentence.

Grammar: Complex Sentences

A complex sentence contains at least one main clause and one or more subordinate clauses.

A main clause has a subject and a predicate and can stand alone as a sentence.

A subordinate clause has a subject and a predicate, but it cannot stand alone as a sentence. It depends on the main clause to complete its meaning. A subordinate clause is usually introduced by a subordinating conjunction, such as *when, because, before,* or *after*.

Complex Sentence	Main Clause	Subordinate Clauses
I was reaching for a puzzle part that was just blue sky when a flash of light filled the bay window. *A Long Way from Chicago*	I was reaching for a puzzle part	that was just blue sky when a flash of light filled the bay window.
I don't even have any friends because I had to leave them all behind when we moved here from Watley. *Because of Winn-Dixie*	I don't even have any friends	because I had to leave them all behind when we moved here from Watley.

Please note that excerpts and passages in the StudySync® library and this workbook are intended as touchstones to generate interest in an author's work. The excerpts and passages do not substitute for the reading of entire texts, and StudySync® strongly recommends that students seek out and purchase the whole literary or informational work in order to experience it as the author intended. Links to online resellers are available in our digital library. In addition, complete works may be ordered through an authorized reseller by filling out and returning to StudySync® the order form enclosed in this workbook.

Reading & Writing Companion

135

⟳ YOUR TURN

1. How could this sentence be changed into a complex sentence?

> People enjoy this custom, but most do not believe in it.

- ○ A. Replace the comma and **but** with a semicolon.
- ○ B. Remove the comma.
- ○ C. Replace the comma and conjunction **but** with **although**.
- ○ D. No change needs to be made to this sentence.

2. How could this sentence be changed into a simple sentence?

> Groundhogs eat large amounts of food before they hibernate.

- ○ A. Place **before they hibernate** followed by a comma before **groundhogs**.
- ○ B. Remove **before they hibernate**.
- ○ C. Remove **Groundhogs eat large amounts of food**.
- ○ D. No change needs to be made to this sentence.

3. How could this sentence be changed into a simple sentence?

> Groundhogs are able to sleep for most of the winter because the food they have eaten turns to fat.

- ○ A. Remove **for most of the winter**.
- ○ B. Remove **because the food they have eaten turns to fat**.
- ○ C. Insert a comma before **because**.
- ○ D. No change needs to be made to this sentence.

4. How could this sentence be changed into a complex sentence?

> Groundhogs come out of their holes to look for food, and they stop to listen for signs of danger.

- ○ A. Replace the comma and conjunction **and** with a semicolon.
- ○ B. Remove the comma and **and they stop to listen for signs of danger**.
- ○ C. Remove the conjunction **and**, then add the subordinating conjunction *when* before **groundhogs**.
- ○ D. No change needs to be made to this sentence.

Literary Analysis Writing Process: Edit and Publish

| PLAN | DRAFT | REVISE | EDIT AND PUBLISH |

You have revised your literary analysis based on your peer feedback and your own examination.

Now, it is time to edit your literary analysis. When you revised, you focused on the content of your literary analysis. You probably looked at the thesis statement, reasons and relevant evidence, introduction, and conclusion. When you edit, you should focus on grammar and punctuation.

Use the checklist below to guide you as you edit:

☐ Have I used sentences of varying lengths and structures, including complex and simple sentences?

☐ Have I used noun clauses correctly?

☐ Have I used adjective clauses correctly?

☐ Do I have any sentence fragments or run-on sentences?

☐ Have I spelled everything correctly?

Notice some edits Knox has made:

- Varied sentence length and structure by combining two sentences into one complex sentence.

- Fixed spelling.

- Varied sentence length and structure by creating two sentences out of one.

- Added a comma to use an adjective clause correctly.

Please note that excerpts and passages in the StudySync® library and this workbook are intended as touchstones to generate interest in an author's work. The excerpts and passages do not substitute for the reading of entire texts, and StudySync® strongly recommends that students seek out and purchase the whole literary or informational work in order to experience it as the author intended. Links to online resellers are available in our digital library. In addition, complete works may be ordered through an authorized reseller by filling out and returning to StudySync® the order form enclosed in this workbook.

Reading & Writing Companion

137

The poem "Annabel Lee" takes a darker turn ~~and showed how the speaker's focus on a relationship makes him irrational. In this poem,~~ because Edgar Allan Poe explores the irrational thoughts of a speaker mourning his departed love. The speaker's love for Annabel Lee is so powerful that he believes it makes angels jealous: "The angels, not half so happy in Heaven, / Went envying her and me—." The speaker shows extreme devotion to his relationship, even after the death of ~~Annabe lee~~ Annabel Lee. "And neither the angels in Heaven above / Nor the demons down under the sea / Can ever dissever my soul from the soul / Of the beautiful Annabel Lee." This poetic statement shows that the speaker does not move on from Annabel Lee after losing her. ~~; and~~ He also holds on to the relationship to make it everlasting. "For the moon never beams, without bringing me dreams / Of the beautiful Annabel Lee." The speaker expresses that deep relationships of love can extend beyond any ~~loss which~~ loss, which includes the profound loss of death. The speaker learns that he cannot move on without Annabel Lee, so his love dominates his thoughts.

✏ WRITE

Use the questions on the previous page, as well as your peer reviews, to help you evaluate your literary analysis to determine areas that need editing. Then edit your narrative to correct those errors.

Once you have made all your corrections, you are ready to publish your work. You can distribute your writing to family and friends, hang it on a bulletin board, or post it on your blog. If you publish online, share the link with your family, friends, and classmates.

Deep Water

FICTION

Introduction

For best friends Elizabeth and Sophie, swimming is the most important part of their lives. For years, they trained together, working hard to reach their goals. Now, at age 17, they both want the only spot available on a top swim team. How will they prepare for the competition? Who will be good enough to make

 VOCABULARY

enthusiasm
great interest and excitement

inevitably
predictably; unavoidably

performance
process of achieving a goal

propel
to move forward

slot
a position in a group or team

NOTES

≡ READ

1   Elizabeth and Sophie shared everything, especially their **enthusiasm** for swimming. At age 17, their identities began and ended with the word "swimmer." The girls competed with each other, their teammates, and their personal best times.

2   When they first began swimming, Sophie had to struggle to keep up. She worked very hard. She trained long hours to improve her **performance**. Elizabeth was as fierce as a coach. She helped with workouts. The girls spent hours lifting weights. They swam at least eight miles a week. Their competition, focus, and determination increased. Both dreamed of being on Team USA, the swim team that competed internationally.

3   At last, they were to compete in the most important swim meet of their lives. The winner would qualify for Team USA. Only one **slot** was available. Only one girl would make the team. The other competitors would not.

4   It was two weeks before the event. The girls felt a distance growing between them.

5   "We need to talk," Elizabeth declared.

6   "It's about the meet, right?" Sophie said. "We have been working hard and training together. It's not about us anymore. It's about me. It's about you. It's about winning."

7   "You're right," Elizabeth said. "I think it would be better if we train separately."

8   The girls chose different times for training. Although time in the pool **inevitably** overlapped, they swam in widely separated lanes.

9   Elizabeth and Sophie made it to the finals, along with Bethany, another member of their team.

10 The competition began. The girls pushed off the side of the pool. Elizabeth was vaguely aware of Sophie and Bethany. Her focus was on moving through the water as effortlessly as a shark. She **propelled** herself 15 meters before surfacing.

11 Sophie flexed and moved smoothly.

12 In the last lap, each girl pushed herself to reach the other side of the pool. When they surfaced, the roar of the crowd was deafening. The judges wanted to see the video of the finish to determine the true winner. Elizabeth and Sophie looked at each other. They clambered out of the pool and hugged. Then they headed for the locker room. They left before the announcement.

13 "Ladies and gentlemen, the winner of the race and new member of Team USA is..."

Please note that excerpts and passages in the StudySync® library and this workbook are intended as touchstones to generate interest in an author's work. The excerpts and passages do not substitute for the reading of entire texts, and StudySync® strongly recommends that students seek out and purchase the whole literary or informational work in order to experience it as the author intended. Links to online resellers are available in our digital library. In addition, complete works may be ordered through an authorized reseller by filling out and returning to StudySync® the order form enclosed in this workbook.

Reading & Writing Companion   141

First Read

Read the story. After you read, answer the Think Questions below.

☁ THINK QUESTIONS

1. What are the names of the two girls at the beginning of the story? What is their relationship?

    The names of the girls are _____.

    They are _____.

2. What do the two girls spend most of their time doing?

    The girls spend their time _____.

3. How does the girls' relationship change two weeks before the important event?

    The girls' relationship changes _____.

4. Use context to confirm the meaning of the word *slot* as it is used in "Deep Water." Write your definition of *slot* here.

    Slot means _____.

    A context clue is _____.

5. What is another way to say that the plane *propelled* through the air?

    The plane_____.

Skill:
Analyzing Expressions

⭐ DEFINE

When you read, you may find English expressions that you do not know. An **expression** is a group of words that communicates an idea. Three types of expressions are idioms, sayings, and figurative language. They can be difficult to understand because the meanings of the words are different from their **literal**, or usual, meanings.

An **idiom** is an expression that is commonly known among a group of people. For example: "It's raining cats and dogs" means it is raining heavily. **Sayings** are short expressions that contain advice or wisdom. For instance: "Don't count your chickens before they hatch" means do not plan on something good happening before it happens. **Figurative** language is when you describe something by comparing it with something else, either directly (using the words *like* or *as*) or indirectly. For example, "I'm as hungry as a horse" means I'm very hungry. None of the expressions are about actual animals.

••• CHECKLIST FOR ANALYZING EXPRESSIONS

To determine the meaning of an expression, remember the following:

✓ If you find a confusing group of words, it may be an expression. The meaning of words in expressions may not be their literal meaning.

- Ask yourself: Is this confusing because the words are new? Or because the words do not make sense together?

✓ Determining the overall meaning may require that you use one or more of the following:

- context clues
- a dictionary or other resource
- teacher or peer support

✓ Highlight important information before and after the expression to look for clues.

YOUR TURN

Read paragraphs 10–12 from "Deep Water." Then, complete the multiple-choice questions below.

> **from "Deep Water"**
>
> The competition began. The girls pushed off the side of the pool. Elizabeth was vaguely aware of Sophie and Bethany. Her focus was on moving through the water as effortlessly as a shark. She propelled herself 15 meters before surfacing.
>
> Sophie flexed and moved smoothly.
>
> In the last lap, each girl pushed herself to reach the other side of the pool. When they surfaced, the roar of the crowd was deafening. The judges wanted to see the video of the finish to determine the true winner. Elizabeth and Sophie looked at each other. They clambered out of the pool and hugged. Then they headed for the locker room. They left before the announcement.

1. At the start of paragraph 12, the expression "pushed herself" means:

   ○ A. used her hand to push against her body

   ○ B. stopped someone

   ○ C. pressed against the end of the pool

   ○ D. tried hard

2. Which context clue helped you determine the meaning of "pushed herself"?

   ○ A. "each girl"

   ○ B. "In the last lap"

   ○ C. "When they surfaced"

   ○ D. "moved smoothly"

Skill:
Sharing Information

 ★ DEFINE

Sharing information involves asking for and giving information. The process of sharing information with other students can help all students learn more and better understand a text or a topic. You can share information when you participate in **brief** discussions or **extended** speaking assignments.

••• CHECKLIST FOR SHARING INFORMATION

When you have to speak for an extended period of time, as in a discussion, you ask for and share information. To ask for and share information, you may use the following sentence frames:

✓ To ask for information:

- What do you think about _____?

- Do you agree that _____?

- What is your understanding of _____?

✓ To give information:

- I think _____.

- I agree because _____.

- My understanding is _____.

Please note that excerpts and passages in the StudySync® library and this workbook are intended as touchstones to generate interest in an author's work. The excerpts and passages do not substitute for the reading of entire texts, and StudySync® strongly recommends that students seek out and purchase the whole literary or informational work in order to experience it as the author intended. Links to online resellers are available in our digital library. In addition, complete works may be ordered through an authorized reseller by filling out and returning to StudySync® the order form enclosed in this workbook.

Reading & Writing Companion   **145**

⟳ YOUR TURN

Watch the "Amigo Brothers" StudySyncTV episode ▶. After watching, sort the following statements from the episode into the appropriate columns:

	Statements
A	He is the one to bring up the problem. And he suggests the solution.
B	It's fighting. I thought these guys were all about not doing that.
C	And they go jogging together every morning.
D	Why do it?
E	What's wrong with boxing?
F	So you think Felix is the leader?

Asking for Information	Giving Information

Close Read

✏️ **WRITE**

NARRATIVE: Think about what happens in the story. Finish the final sentence and explain what happens next. Who wins? How do Elizabeth and Sophie react? Pay attention to the *IE* and *EI* spelling rules as you write.

Use the checklist below to guide you as you write.

☐ Who wins the race?

☐ How do Elizabeth and Sophie react?

☐ What happened in the story to lead to the loser's reaction?

Use the sentence frames to organize and write your narrative.

"Ladies and gentlemen, the winner of the race and new member of Team USA is _____

_____."

At that moment, Sophie _____

_____.

Then Elizabeth _____

_____.

In the end, _____

_____.

Sarah's Neighbor

FICTION

Introduction

Set in San Francisco shortly after the bombing of Pearl Harbor during World War II, this short story focuses on a preteen girl's struggle to accept her parents' changing attitudes toward their Japanese neighbors, including her best friend, Ayako. As twelve-year-old Sarah watches Ayako through the window, she longs to rekindle their friendship—but she is too scared of her father to disobey.

VOCABULARY

erupt
to burst suddenly

clasp
to hold tightly

badge
a small pin or patch that gives information about the person wearing it

symbol
an object that represents an idea

Training
developing the skills
employees need to perf
improve their performanc
skills, and abilities, speci

accentuate
to call attention to something

vibrate
to shake

authority
power; being the leader

READ

NOTES

1   Sarah looked through the window as she did the dishes. Ayako, her neighbor and former best friend, sat on the swing set outside. She looked as lonely as a ghost. Sarah would have been delighted to drop the silverware and **erupt** through the door to join Ayako. But she knew she couldn't. Her mind flashed to the conversation she had with her parents a few weeks ago, after the Japanese attacked Pearl Harbor.

2   Her father had come home from an arduous shift at the San Francisco police department. People were angry about the bombing. There had been fighting in the streets. They couldn't trust the Japanese anymore—not even Ayako.

He pulled out his sergeant's **badge**. He began polishing it as a way of **accentuating** his **authority**. "That girl and her family are the enemy," he'd said.

3   Later, Sarah asked her mother to explain. It didn't make any sense. The bombing of Pearl Harbor was a serious attack. But Ayako hadn't been a part of it. Her mother **clasped** Sarah's hand. "Ayako didn't do anything bad. But she's a **symbol** of the people who did. The sergeant has given you orders. It's best you follow them."

4   Sarah grabbed a plate off the stack and focused on the circular movement of washing. She glued her eyes to the plate to take her mind off Ayako. There would be a harsh penalty if she asked to go play with her friend. Trepidation kept her mouth closed.

5   The next morning, Sarah and her mother made a list of guests for her thirteenth birthday party. Her mother named each child from Sarah's class, and Sarah wrote them down. Then she had an idea. Tightening her grip on the pencil, she urgently sneaked another name into the middle of the list: Ayako's.

6   As she handed the list to her mother, her father came in. He scanned the list over his wife's shoulder. When he got to Ayako's name, he **vibrated** with rage.

7   He faced Sarah and growled. "How many times have I told you that this girl cannot be your friend? I will not have my daughter spending time with someone like her! You will never see this girl again, or I will never see you again. Understand?"

8   Sarah wanted to stand up for herself. She wanted to tell her father that he was wrong, that Ayako is a good person. But all that came out was silence.

First Read

Read the story. After you read, answer the Think Questions below.

☁ **THINK QUESTIONS**

1. Who is Sarah's neighbor?

   Sarah's neighbor is _____.

2. What event changes Sarah's relationship with her neighbor?

   Sarah's relationship with her neighbor changes _____.

3. What did Sarah do to the list of guests for her birthday party?

   Sarah _____.

4. Use context to confirm the meaning of the word *symbol* as it is used in "Sarah's Neighbor." Write your definition of *symbol* here.

   Symbol means _____.

   A context clue is _____.

5. What is another way to say a mother *clasps* her daughter's hand?

   A mother _____.

Please note that excerpts and passages in the StudySync® library and this workbook are intended as touchstones to generate interest in an author's work. The excerpts and passages do not substitute for the reading of entire texts, and StudySync® strongly recommends that students seek out and purchase the whole literary or informational work in order to experience it as the author intended. Links to online resellers are available in our digital library. In addition, complete works may be ordered through an authorized reseller by filling out and returning to StudySync® the order form enclosed in this workbook.

Reading & Writing Companion 151

Skill:
Language Structures

★ DEFINE

In every language, there are rules that tell how to **structure** sentences. These rules define the correct order of words. In the English language, for example, a **basic** structure for sentences is subject, verb, and object. Some sentences have more **complicated** structures.

You will encounter both basic and complicated **language structures** in the classroom materials you read. Being familiar with language structures will help you better understand the text.

••• CHECKLIST FOR LANGUAGE STRUCTURES

To improve your comprehension of language structures, do the following:

✓ Monitor your understanding.

- Ask yourself: Why do I not understand this sentence? Is it because I do not understand some of the words? Or is it because I do not understand the way the words are ordered in the sentence?

✓ Break down the sentence into its parts.

- In English, adjectives almost always come before the noun. Example: He had a **big dog.**

  > A **noun** names a person, place, thing, or idea.

  > An **adjective** modifies, or describes, a noun or a pronoun.

  > If there is more than one adjective, they usually appear in the following order separated by a comma: quantity or number, quality or opinion, size, age, shape, color.

    Example: He had a **big, brown dog.**

  > If there is more than one adjective from the same category, include the word *and.*

    Example: He had a **brown and white dog.**

- Ask yourself: What are the nouns in this sentence? What adjectives describe them? In what order are the nouns and adjectives?

✓ Confirm your understanding with a peer or teacher.

YOUR TURN

Read each sentence in the first column. Then, complete the chart by writing the words and phrases into the "Adjective" and "Noun" columns. The first row has been done as an example.

Sentence	Adjective	Noun
Her father had come home from an arduous shift at the San Francisco police department.	arduous	shift
The bombing of Pearl Harbor was a serious attack.		
Sarah grabbed a plate off the stack and focused on the circular movement of washing.		
There would be a harsh penalty if she asked to go play with her friend.		
She wanted to tell her father that he was wrong, that Ayako is a good person.		

Skill: Developing Background Knowledge

★ DEFINE

Developing background knowledge is the process of gaining information about different topics. By developing your background knowledge, you will be able to better understand a wider variety of texts.

First, preview the text to determine what the text is about. To **preview** the text, read the title, headers, and other text features and look at any images or graphics. As you are previewing, identify anything that is unfamiliar to you and that seems important.

While you are reading, you can look for clues that will help you learn more about any unfamiliar words, phrases, or topics. You can also look up information in another resource to increase your background knowledge.

••• CHECKLIST FOR DEVELOPING BACKGROUND KNOWLEDGE

To develop your background knowledge, do the following:

- ✓ Preview the text. Read the title, headers, and other features. Look at any images and graphics.

- ✓ Identify any words, phrases, or topics that you do not know a lot about.

- ✓ As you are reading, try to find clues in the text that give you information about any unfamiliar words, phrases, or topics.

- ✓ If necessary, look up information in other sources to learn more about any unfamiliar words, phrases, or topics. You can also ask a peer or teacher for information or support.

- ✓ Think about how the background knowledge you have gained helps you better understand the text.

YOUR TURN

Read paragraphs 2–3 from "Sarah's Neighbor." Then, complete the multiple-choice questions below.

---

from **"Sarah's Neighbor"**

Her father had come home from an arduous shift at the San Francisco police department. People were angry about the bombing. There had been fighting in the streets. They couldn't trust the Japanese anymore—not even Ayako. He pulled out his sergeant's badge. He began polishing it as a way of accentuating his authority. "That girl and her family are the enemy," he'd said.

Later, Sarah asked her mother to explain. It didn't make any sense. The bombing of Pearl Harbor was a serious attack. But Ayako hadn't been a part of it. Her mother clasped Sarah's hand. "Ayako didn't do anything bad. But she's a symbol of the people who did. The sergeant has given you orders. It's best you follow them."

---

1. The details in paragraph 2 show that Americans:

    ○ A. were upset and mad at the Japanese.

    ○ B. were scared of the police.

    ○ C. were tired.

    ○ D. wanted to fight families that had daughters.

2. Clues that best develop this background knowledge are:

    ○ A. "arduous shift" and "San Francisco police department"

    ○ B. "angry at the bombing," "fighting in the streets," and "couldn't trust the Japanese"

    ○ C. "sergeant's badge," "polishing," and "accentuating his authority"

    ○ D. "not even Ayako," "That girl and her family," and "the enemy"

3. Sarah's conversation with her mother shows that:

    ○ A Americans were not affected by World War II.

    ○ B. Americans believed that Ayako's family caused the attack.

    ○ C. some people thought the treatment of Japanese-Americans was unfair.

    ○ D. Americans did not understand what happened at Pearl Harbor.

4. A detail that best develops this background knowledge is:

    ○ A. "Her mother clasped Sarah's hand."

    ○ B. "The bombing of Pearl Harbor was a serious attack."

    ○ C. "'Ayako didn't do anything bad.'"

    ○ D. "'The sergeant has given you orders.'"

Please note that excerpts and passages in the StudySync® library and this workbook are intended as touchstones to generate interest in an author's work. The excerpts and passages do not substitute for the reading of entire texts, and StudySync® strongly recommends that students seek out and purchase the whole literary or informational work in order to experience it as the author intended. Links to online resellers are available in our digital library. In addition, complete works may be ordered through an authorized reseller by filling out and returning to StudySync® the order form enclosed in this workbook.

Reading & Writing Companion   **155**

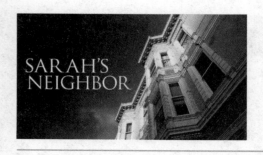

Close Read

Copyright © Bookheaded Learning, LLC

 WRITE

LITERARY ANALYSIS: How has Sarah's life changed since the bombing of Pearl Harbor? Write a short paragraph in which you explain what her life was like before and what it is like now. Pay attention to matching pronouns and antecedents as you write.

Use the checklist below to guide you as you write.

☐ What was Sarah's life like before the bombing of Pearl Harbor?

☐ What is different about Sarah's life after the bombing of Pearl Harbor?

☐ What are the reasons for the changes in Sarah's life?

☐ How does Sarah feel about the changes in her life?

Use the sentence frames to organize and write your literary analysis.

The bombing of Pearl Harbor was an attack during _____

by the Japanese military against the United States.

Before the bombing of Pearl Harbor, Sarah's best friend was her Japanese-American _____

_____, Ayako.

After Pearl Harbor, Sarah is not _____ to see Ayako.

Sarah's father says that Ayako is an _____ of the country.

Sarah believes that Ayako is a _____.

PHOTO/IMAGE CREDITS:

cover, iStock.com/PKM1
cover, ©iStock.com/eyewave, ©iStock.com/subjug,
©iStock.com/lvantsov, iStock.com/borchee, ©iStock.com/
seb_ra
p. iii, iStock.com/DNY59
p. iv, iStock.com/EcoPic
p. v, iStock.com/EcoPic
p. v, iStock.com/deimagine
p. vi, iStock.com/EcoPic
p. vi, ©iStock.com/Avalon_Studio
p. vi, iStock.com/dageldog
p. vi, iStock/AndreyPopov
p. vi, Mordolff/iStock
p. vi, IS_ImageSource/iStock
p. vii, iStock.com/hanibaram, iStock.com/seb_ra, iStock.
com/Martin Barraud
p. vii, iStock.com/oonal
p. ix, iStock.com/PKM1
p. x, Charles Dickens - London Stereoscopic Company/
Stringer/Hulton Archive/Getty
p. x, Albert Marrin - JIM WATSON/Staff/AFP/Getty
p. x, Alfred Noyes - E. O. Hoppe/Contributor/The LIFE
Picture Collection/Getty Images
p. x, Edgar Allen Poe - Universal History Archive/
Contributor/Universal Images Group/Getty Images
p. x, Susan Power - Raphael GAILLARDE/Contributor/
Gamma-Rapho/Getty Images
p. 0, iStock.com/Diane Labombarbe
p. 1, Culture Club/Hulton Archive/Getty Images
p. 3, iStock.com/Diane Labombarbe
p. 4, iStock.com/
p. 5, iStock.com/
p. 6, iStock.com/fotogaby
p. 7, iStock.com/fotogaby
p. 8, iStock.com/Hohenhaus
p. 9, iStock.com/Hohenhaus
p. 10, iStock.com/Diane Labombarbe
p. 11, iStock.com/dmfoss
p. 14, iStock.com/ImagineGolf
p. 18, iStock.com/ImagineGolf
p. 19, iStock.com/donatas1205
p. 20, iStock.com/donatas1206
p. 21, iStock.com/fotogaby
p. 22, iStock.com/fotogaby
p. 23, iStock.com/ImagineGolf
p. 24, iStock.com/Floortje
p. 38, iStock.com/Floortje
p. 39, iStock.com/Gemini-Create
p. 40, iStock.com/Gemini-Create
p. 41, istock.com/urbancow
p. 42, istock.com/urbancow
p. 43, iStock.com/Floortje
p. 44, iStock.com/WLDavies
p. 46, iStock.com/WLDavies
p. 47, iStock.com/
p. 48, iStock.com/
p. 49, iStock.com/WLDavies
p. 50, iStock.com/cmannphoto
p. 51, StudySync
p. 52, StudySync
p. 53, StudySync
p. 56, iStock.com/cmannphoto

p. 57, iStock.com/ThomasVogel
p. 58, iStock.com/ThomasVogel
p. 59, iStock.com/cmannphoto
p. 60, iStock.com/Paul Grecaud
p. 61, Universal History Archive/Univeral Images Group/
Getty Images
p. 65, iStock.com/Paul Grecaud
p. 66, iStock.com/
p. 67, iStock.com/
p. 69, iStock.com/Hohenhaus
p. 70, iStock.com/Hohenhaus
p. 72, iStock.com/Paul Grecaud
p. 73, iStock.com/
p. 74, Hulton Archive/Archive Photos/Getty Images
p. 78, iStock.com/
p. 79, iStock.com/Caval
p. 80, iStock.com/Caval
p. 81, iStock.com/
p. 82, iStock.com/Liliboas
p. 87, iStock.com/Anastasiia_Guseva
p. 92, iStock.com/phaitoons
p. 95, iStock.com/phaitoons
p. 96, iStock.com/Martin Barraud
p. 97, iStock.com/Martin Barraud
p. 98, iStock.com/phaitoons
p. 99, iStock.com/hanibaram, iStock.com/seb_ra, iStock.
com/Martin Barraud
p. 100, iStock.com/Martin Barraud
p. 106, iStock.com/gopixa
p. 108, iStock.com/fstop123
p. 111, iStock.com/domin_domin
p. 114, iStock.com/Martin Barraud
p. 119, iStock.com/bo1982
p. 121, iStock.com/Jeff_Hu
p. 124, iStock.com/Fodor90
p. 127, iStock.com/stevedangers
p. 129, iStock.com/Martin Barraud
p. 131, iStock.com/
p. 133, iStock.com/
p. 135, ©iStock.com/wildpixel
p. 137, iStock.com/Martin Barraud
p. 139, iStock.com/stanley45
p. 140, stevecoleimages/iStock
p. 140, PeopleImages/iStock
p. 140, goodynewshoes/iStock
p. 140, abadonian/iStock
p. 140, iStock.com/
p. 142, iStock.com/stanley45
p. 143, iStock.com/Ales_Utovko
p. 145, iStock.com/Zoran Kolundzija
p. 147, iStock.com/stanley45
p. 148, iStock.com/halbergman
p. 149, Todor Tsvetkov/iStock
p. 149, kickimages/iStock
p. 149, jtgriffin07/iStock
p. 149, typhoonski/iStock
p. 149, Beboy_ltd/iStock
p. 149, Straitshooter/iStock
p. 149, choness/iStock
p. 151, iStock.com/halbergman
p. 152, iStock.com/BlackJack3D
p. 154, iStock.com/Mlenny
p. 156, iStock.com/halbergman

Text Fulfillment
Through StudySync

If you are interested in specific titles, please fill out the form below and we will check availability through our partners.

ORDER DETAILS

Date:

TITLE	AUTHOR	Paperback/Hardcover	Specific Edition *If Applicable*	Quantity

SHIPPING INFORMATION

Contact:

Title:

School/District:

Address Line 1:

Address Line 2:

Zip or Postal Code:

Phone:

Mobile:

Email:

BILLING INFORMATION　☐ *SAME AS SHIPPING*

Contact:

Title:

School/District:

Address Line 1:

Address Line 2:

Zip or Postal Code:

Phone:

Mobile:

Email:

PAYMENT INFORMATION

☐ CREDIT CARD   Name on Card:

Card Number:　　　Expiration Date:　　　Security Code:

☐ PO   Purchase Order Number:

StudySync Text Fulfillment, BookheadEd Learning, LLC
610 Daniel Young Drive | Sonoma, CA 95476